123 Homemade Ravioli Recipes

(123 Homemade Ravioli Recipes - Volume 1)

Maria Harris

Copyright: Published in the United States by Maria Harris/ © MARIA HARRIS

Published on November, 19 2020

All rights reserved. No part of this publication may be reproduced, stored in retrieval system, copied in any form or by any means, electronic, mechanical, photocopying, recording or otherwise transmitted without written permission from the publisher. Please do not participate in or encourage piracy of this material in any way. You must not circulate this book in any format. MARIA HARRIS does not control or direct users' actions and is not responsible for the information or content shared, harm and/or actions of the book readers.

In accordance with the U.S. Copyright Act of 1976, the scanning, uploading and electronic sharing of any part of this book without the permission of the publisher constitute unlawful piracy and theft of the author's intellectual property. If you would like to use material from the book (other than just simply for reviewing the book), prior permission must be obtained by contacting the author at author@cuminrecipes.com

Thank you for your support of the author's rights.

Content

123 AWESOME RAVIOLI RECIPES............ 5

1. Alfredo Ravioli Bake Recipe 5
2. Baked Ravioli Recipe 5
3. Baked Spinacotta Cheese Ravioli Recipe 6
4. Bean Amp Spinach Ravioli Recipe............... 6
5. Beefy Spinach Ravioli Recipe 7
6. Buffalo Ravioli Recipe 7
7. Butternut Squash Ravioli With Sage Butter And Walnuts Recipe 7
8. Chads 4 Cheese Ravioli Crawfish Alfredo Recipe 8
9. Cheese Ravioli With Pumpkin Sauce Recipe 8
10. Cheese Ravioli With Toasted Walnuts Recipe 9
11. Cheese Ravioli And Spinach Salad Recipe .. 9
12. Chevre And Spinach Wonton Ravioli With Fresh Parsley Sauce Recipe 10
13. Chicken Alfredo Ravioli Bake Recipe 10
14. Chicken Marsala Ravioli Recipe................ 11
15. Chicken Amp Spinach Ravioli Recipe 11
16. Chinese Dumplings Recipe 12
17. Crab And Smoked Salmon Ravioli Recipe 12
18. Crabmeat Ravioli Recipe............................ 13
19. Crabmeat Ravioli With Clam Sauce Recipe 14
20. Creamy Chicken N Roasted Garlic Ravioli Lasagna Two Ways Recipe 14
21. Denny's Sausage And Ricotta Ravioli Recipe 15
22. Easy Baked Ravioli Recipe 16
23. Easy Homemade Ravioli Recipe 16
24. Easy Ravioli No Need For A Pasta Machine Recipe 16
25. Easy Ravioli Bake Recipe.......................... 17
26. Easy Ravioli Casserole Recipe................... 17
27. Eggplant Ravioli Filling Recipe 18
28. Elaines Homemade Beef N Cheese Ravioli Recipe 18
29. Feta Cheese Ravioli With Yellow Pepper Sauce Recipe... 20
30. Fiesta Ravioli Recipe 20
31. Foie Gras Ravioli With Port Currant Reduction Recipe... 20
32. Fresh English Pea Ravioli With Salsa Verde Recipe.. 21
33. Fried Ravioli Recipe 22
34. Gluten Free Cheese Raviolis Recipe 23
35. Gorgonzola Cream Sauce............................ 23
36. Grammys Raviolis Recipe.......................... 24
37. Greek Style Beef And Cheese Ravioli Recipe.. 24
38. Ham And Leek Ravioli Recipe...................24
39. Hearty Ravioli Recipe 25
40. Homemade Mushroom And Ricotta Ravioli Recipe.. 26
41. In Side Out Ravioli Recipe 26
42. Inside Out Ravioli Recipe 26
43. Italian Pork Ravioli Filling Recipe 27
44. Kathleens Sage Brown Butter Ravioli Recipe.. 28
45. Leftover Ravioli Recipe 28
46. Lobster Ravioli With Mascarpone Cream Sauce Recipe... 28
47. Maltese Ravioli Recipe 29
48. Manti Turkish Ravioli With Yogurt Sauce Recipe.. 29
49. Mock Ravioli Recipe 30
50. Mushroom And Chestnut Raviolis Recipe 30
51. Mushroom Ravioli Recipe.......................... 31
52. Mushroom Ravioli Stuffing Recipe 31
53. Mushroom And Cheese Ravioli With Smoked Tomato Cream Sauce Recipe 31
54. Olive Garden Cheese Ravioli With Fresh Vegetables Recipe 33
55. Otterpond Sausage Ravioli Recipe 33
56. Pelmeni Russian Ravioli Recipe 34
57. Pesto Ravioli With Goat Cheese And Walnuts Recipe.. 34
58. Philly Cheesesteak Ravioli Recipe............. 35
59. Portobello Mushroom Ravioli With Prawns Recipe.. 36
60. Potato Ravioli With Braised Leeks And Potato Crisp Recipe 36
61. Pumpkin Ravioli Recipe 37
62. Pumpkin Ravioli W Hazelnut Cream Recipe 38
63. Pumpkin Raviolis Recipe 39
64. Pumpkin Seed Pesto With Pumpkin Ravioli Recipe.. 39

65. Quick Ravioli Bake Recipe 40
66. Ravioli Alfredo With Shrimp Recipe 40
67. Ravioli Casserole Recipe 41
68. Ravioli Casserole In The Crockpot Recipe 41
69. Ravioli Lasagna Recipe 41
70. Ravioli Lasange Recipe 42
71. Ravioli Marinara Recipe 42
72. Ravioli Skillet Lasagna Florentine Recipe . 42
73. Ravioli Skillet Recipe 43
74. Ravioli With Balsamic Butter Recipe 43
75. Ravioli With Brown Butter And Sage Recipe 43
76. Ravioli With Creamy Pesto Sauce Recipe . 44
77. Ravioli With Gorgonzola Artichoke Hearts And Peas Sauce Recipe 44
78. Ravioli With Spinach Alfredo Recipe 45
79. Ravioli With Spinach Chicken And Ricotta Recipe 45
80. Ravioli With Zucchini And Walnuts Recipe 46
81. Ravioli And Sausage Lasagna Recipe 46
82. Ravioli Con Ricotta E Spinaci Ravioli Stuffed With Spinach And Ricotta Cheese Recipe 47
83. Ravioli In Pinon Cream Sauce Recipe 47
84. Ravioli With Balsamic Brown Butter Recipe 48
85. Ravioli With Corn Recipe 48
86. Ravioli With Northwest Pesto Sauce Recipe 49
87. Ravioli With Nutty Cream Sauce Recipe .. 49
88. Ravioli With Oil And Garlic Recipe 49
89. Ravioli With Roasted Squash And Sage Brown Butter Recipe 50
90. Raviolis Stuffed With Beemster XO Recipe 50
91. Ravoli With Fresh Sage Butter Recipe 51
92. Roasted Butternut Squash Ravioli Recipe. 51
93. Roasted Winter Squash Ravioli With Sausage Cream Sauce Recipe 51
94. SEAFOOD STUFFED RAVIOLI Recipe 52
95. SPINACH RAVIOLI LASAGNA Recipe 53
96. Sausage And Ravioli In Garlic And Olive Oil Recipe 53

97. Seafood Ravioli With White Wine Sauce Recipe 54
98. Seared Scallops Mango Ravioli Prosciutto Parsnip Chips Balsamic Pomegranate Reduction Recipe 55
99. Shiitake Pumpkin Ravioli Recipe 55
100. Sicilian Ricotta Ravioli Filling Recipe 56
101. Simone Remoli's Father's Day Meaty Treat: Oxtail Ravioli Recipe 56
102. Slow Cooker Cheesy Ravioli Casserole Recipe 57
103. Slow Cooker Ravioli Lasagna Recipe 57
104. Smoked Salmon Ravioli Recipe 58
105. Speedy Chicken And Ravioli Recipe 58
106. Spicy Beef And Sausage Ravioli With Ariabatta Sauce Recipe 59
107. Spicy Spinach And Cheese Ravioli Recipe 59
108. Spinach And Ravioli Recipe 60
109. Spinach Garlic Ravioli Recipe 60
110. Spinach Ravioli Recipe 61
111. Sweet Potato Ravioli With Lemon Sage Brown Butter Recipe 61
112. TEX MEX MINI RAVIOLI SOUP Recipe 62
113. Taco Ravioli Bake Recipe 62
114. Toasted Ravioli Puffs 62
115. Tomatoes And Ravioli With Escarole Recipe 63
116. Venison Wonton Ravioli Recipe 63
117. White Bean Ravioli With Brown Butter And Caper Sauce Recipe 64
118. Zesty Cheese Ravioli Recipe 64
119. Asparagus Ravioli In Parmesan Broth Recipe 65
120. Four Cheese Ravioli Recipe 66
121. Ravioli Lasagna Recipe 67
122. Ravioli With Ricotta Sage Filling Recipe ... 67
123. Rock N Roll Ravioli Lazagna Recipe 67

INDEX 69
CONCLUSION 71

123 Awesome Ravioli Recipes

***

1. Alfredo Ravioli Bake Recipe

Serving: 8 | Prep: | Cook: 20mins | Ready in:

Ingredients

- 2 tablespoons LAND O LAKES® butter
- 1 1/4 pounds boneless skinless chicken breast halves, cut into 1-inch pieces
- 1 (8-ounce) package sliced fresh mushrooms
- 1 (16-ounce) jar alfredo sauce
- 1 (25 to 27 1/2-ounce) package frozen cheese-filled ravioli
- 1 large (1 cup) red bell pepper, chopped
- 8 ounces (2 cups) LAND O LAKES® mozzarella cheese, shredded
- 1/4 cup shredded parmesan cheese

Direction

- Heat oven to 350°F. Melt butter in 12-inch skillet until sizzling; add chicken pieces. Cook over medium-high heat until chicken is lightly browned (4 to 6 minutes). Add mushrooms; continue cooking until chicken is no longer pink and mushrooms are tender (4 to 6 minutes). Do not drain.
- Spread 1/2 cup sauce into greased 13x9-inch baking dish. Arrange single layer of frozen ravioli over sauce; drizzle 3/4 cup sauce evenly over ravioli. Spread with 1 1/2 cups chicken and mushroom mixture, 1/2 cup red bell pepper and 1 cup mozzarella cheese. Repeat with remaining ingredients, except remaining 1 cup mozzarella cheese and Parmesan cheese. Cover tightly with aluminum foil. Bake for 45 minutes.
- Remove foil; sprinkle with remaining mozzarella and Parmesan cheese. Bake, uncovered, for 15 to 20 minutes or until cheeses are melted. Let stand 15 minutes before serving.
- TIP: To make ahead, prepare as directed above except do not bake. Cover; refrigerate up to 24 hours. When ready to bake, continue as directed above. Increase first baking time to 1 hour.
- Makes 8 servings
- Nutritional Info Per 1 Serving: Calories 550, Fat 33 g, Cholesterol 125 mg, Sodium 1010 mg, Carbohydrates 30 g, Dietary Fiber 2 g, Protein 35 g
- This recipe created by Land O'Lakes.

2. Baked Ravioli Recipe

Serving: 4 | Prep: | Cook: 45mins | Ready in:

Ingredients

- 2 pounds store-bought frozen ravioli
- 1 1/2 cups shredded mozzarella
- 1/2 cup grated parmesan cheese
- 1 can (28 ounces) whole tomatoes
- 1 can (28 ounces) crushed tomatoes
- 1 medium onion, chopped
- 3 cloves garlic, minced
- coarse salt and freshly ground pepper
- 1 1/2 teaspoons dried thyme, or oregano
- 2 tablespoons olive oil

Direction

- Preheat oven to 425 degrees. Heat oil in a large saucepan over medium heat. Add onion and garlic, and season with salt and pepper; cook, stirring occasionally, until softened, about 5 minutes. Add thyme and tomatoes. Bring to a

- boil, reduce heat, and simmer, breaking up tomatoes with spoon, until sauce is thickened and reduced to about 5 1/2 cups, 20 to 25 minutes.
- Meanwhile, cook ravioli in a large pot of boiling salted water just until they float to the top (pasta will continue to cook in oven). Drain pasta; return to pot.
- Toss sauce with pasta. Pour pasta into a large gratin dish or 9-by-13-inch baking dish, and sprinkle with cheeses. Bake until golden, 20 to 25 minutes. Cool slightly before serving.
- * Obviously also wonderful with ground beef

3. Baked Spinacotta Cheese Ravioli Recipe

Serving: 4 | Prep: | Cook: 30mins | Ready in:

Ingredients

- 250g fresh baby spinach
- 350g cheese ravioli
- 1 cup ricotta cheese
- 2 cups mozza and cheddar cheese shredded blend
- 3 cups pasta sauce (one jar)
- 1 tomato, sliced
- 1 tsp dried basil
- 1 tsp dried oregano
- handful of romano cheese

Direction

- Preheat oven to 400 degrees
- Spray a deep casserole dish or 9x13 dish with non-stick spray
- Layer the bottom of the casserole dish with your baby spinach (leave enough spinach to use for your pasta mixture and the top of your casserole)
- In a large mixing bowl combine your uncooked ravioli, ricotta cheese and pasta sauce and a handful of spinach. Mix well, but gently
- Pour pasta/ravioli mixture into your casserole dish
- Layer your remaining spinach on top
- Sprinkle with the mozzarella and cheese blend (use as much as you like)
- Place your tomato slices on top and sprinkle them with the basil and oregano
- Now add your Romano cheese (also as much as you like)
- Cover with foil (or you can try it with no foil) and bake for 60 minutes, until cheese is nice and bubbly
- Take out, remove foil
- Place back in the oven and broil until cheese is nice and brown
- ****We found with a deep casserole dish we had to bake it at a higher temp, but you can always fiddle around with the temp and time*****
- *****You could always cook the ravioli first, and lower your temperature!! Say 350 for 30 minutes******

4. Bean Amp Spinach Ravioli Recipe

Serving: 3 | Prep: | Cook: 3mins | Ready in:

Ingredients

- 1/2 cup pre-cooked or canned white beans (I cooked my own; used a tsp of becel olive oil marg in the cooking water)
- 50 grams of frozen chopped spinach
- 1/2 cup part skim ricotta cheese
- 30 wonton wrappers

Direction

- Heat a large pot of water. Bring to a boil.
- Meanwhile, defrost the spinach in microwave. Squeeze out excess moisture. Place in food processor with beans & cheese. Process until smooth. You should have approx. 1 cup of filling.

- Spread out wrappers on a counter. Place 1 tsp. of filling on each wrapper. Moisten edges and fold on the diagonal. Seal edges.
- Boil in water for about 2 minutes.
- Top with tomato sauce, diced tomatoes, and/or cheeses. YUM!
- Makes 3 servings of 10 ravioli each.

5. Beefy Spinach Ravioli Recipe

Serving: 4 | Prep: | Cook: 30mins | Ready in:

Ingredients

- 1 pound extra lean ground beef
- 1 medium white onion chopped
- 3 clove garlic minced
- 16 ounces tomato sauce
- 6 ounces tomato paste
- 1 tablespoon dried parsley
- 1/2 teaspoon oregano
- 1/2 teaspoon salt
- 1/2 teaspoon freshly ground black pepper
- 6 ounces rigatoni pasta uncooked
- 10 ounces frozen spinach chopped
- 1 cup cheddar cheese shredded
- 1/2 cup soft bread crumbs
- 2 medium eggs beaten
- 1/4 cup grated parmesan cheese

Direction

- Brown ground beef, garlic and onion in a large skillet then drain off any excess fat.
- Add tomato sauce and tomato paste, parsley, oregano, salt and pepper then simmer 10 minutes.
- Cook pasta according to package directions until just softened but not quite done.
- Drain and rinse with cold water then put back into pan in which it was cooked.
- Add cooked spinach, cheddar cheese, bread crumbs, eggs and parmesan cheese.
- Spread mixture in a rectangular greased baking dish then top with meat mixture.
- Sprinkle more grated parmesan cheese on top then bake at 350 for 30 minutes.

6. Buffalo Ravioli Recipe

Serving: 1 | Prep: | Cook: 2mins | Ready in:

Ingredients

- 1 can Chef Boyardee Overstuffed beef Ravioli
- Frank's Red Hot Buffalo Sauce (some)

Direction

- Spray inside of Tupperware with Pam or coat lightly with oil to prevent staining (or don't if you are lazy)
- Open can of Ravioli and pour into container
- Pour in a generous serving of Frank's Red Hot
- Microwave on high for 2 minutes

7. Butternut Squash Ravioli With Sage Butter And Walnuts Recipe

Serving: 8 | Prep: | Cook: 8mins | Ready in:

Ingredients

- For the Pasta:
- 6 sheets prepared fresh egg pasta (double recipe of below link):
- semolina-pasta.html">Fresh Semolina Pasta
- ~~~~~~~~~~~~~~~~~~~~~~~~~~~~~~~~~~~~~
- For the filling:
- 3 butternut squash, cut in half and roasted with olive oil and kosher salt, until tender
- 1/4 cup mascarpone cheese
- nutmeg, to taste
- kosher salt and white pepper, to taste
- ~~~~~~~~~~~~~~~~~~~~~~~~~~~~~~~~~~~~~
- For the sage butter:

- 12 oz. cold unsalted butter
- 1/2 cup walnut pieces
- 1/3 cup thinly sliced fresh sage leaves
- Kosher salt and black pepper
- Garnish:
- fresh sage leaves
- parmigiano-reggiano cheese, freshly grated

Direction

- After roasting the squash, scoop out the flesh and purée until smooth with the remaining ingredients. Set aside.
- Bring a large pot of salted water to a boil. Lay out three of the pasta sheets and begin placing approximately two tablespoons of the filling about two inches from each other. Place a second sheet over the first and use a ravioli cutter to form squares, making sure that all of the edges are sealed. Cook ravioli in the boiling water, about 3-5 minutes, until al dente.
- Place the cold butter in a medium skillet preheated over medium heat. Do not swirl or move around. Once the butter has melted and has begun to turn brown around the edges, add the sage and salt and pepper to taste.
- To serve, add the ravioli into the hot skillet with the brown butter mixture. When the pasta becomes brown and slightly crispy, remove and serve on a warm platter topped with more thinly sliced sage and freshly grated Parmigiano-Reggiano.

8. Chads 4 Cheese Ravioli Crawfish Alfredo Recipe

Serving: 4 | Prep: | Cook: 30mins | Ready in:

Ingredients

- alfredo sauce Ingredients
- 2 sticks butter
- 2 pints heavy whipping cream
- 1 1/2 cups fresh grated parmesan cheese
- 1 fresh minced garlic clove
- 1 tsp nutmeg
- 1 tsp salt
- 3/4 tsp fresh ground white pepper or regular pepper
- 1 package pre-cooked crawfish
- 1 1/2 pounds of 4 cheese ravioli
- 1/4 cup diced onion
- 1 minced garlic clove
- 1/8 cup EVOO
- 1/8 cup of butter
- 1/8 cup of brown sugar
- Dash of salt, pepper, paprika (and cayenne pepper if desired)

Direction

- ALFREDO SAUCE: On stove top (medium heat) stir continuously until sauce is a medium think consistency. To decrease cooking time you can always buy pre-made Alfredo sauce from the grocery store (I like Butoni)
- Boil Pasta: set aside (boil with plenty of salt and EVOO)
- Sauté 1/4 cup diced onion and 1 minced garlic clove with 1/8 cup EVOO (extra virgin olive oil) until softened
- Increase heat slightly and then: Add craw fish, 1/8 cup butter, 1/8 cup brown sugar, salt, pepper and paprika. Cook until crawfish is lightly browned
- Keep ingredients separate when finished
- To serve: 1st Pasta, 2nd Craw fish, 3rd (MY FAVORITE) Alfredo sauce
- Use lemon wedge and paprika or oregano to garnish if desired and Start making the YUM noise because this one is TOO GOOD!

9. Cheese Ravioli With Pumpkin Sauce Recipe

Serving: 6 | Prep: | Cook: 25mins | Ready in:

Ingredients

- 1 bag (30 ounces) frozen cheese ravioli
- 1 can (15 ounces) solid pack pumpkin
- 1 can (15 ounces) reduced-sodium chicken or vegetable broth
- 3 tablespoons brown sugar
- 1 tablespoon butter or margarine
- 1/2 teaspoon garlic powder
- 1/2 teaspoon ground ginger or 1 teaspoon bottled, minced ginger
- 1/2 teaspoon ground cinnamon
- 1/8 teaspoon ground nutmeg
- 1/4 cup reduced-fat sour cream
- 1/4 cup grated parmesan cheese, optional

Direction

- Preparation Time: Approximately 15 minutes
- Cook Time: Approximately 25 minutes
- Preparation:
- Place a large saucepan of water over high heat. Cover and bring to a boil. When water comes to a boil, add ravioli and cook according to package directions. Drain and set aside. Meanwhile, combine pumpkin, broth, sugar, butter, garlic powder, ginger, cinnamon and nutmeg in a medium saucepan, and stir to combine. Place over medium heat and bring to a simmer, stirring occasionally, until butter melts and mixture is heated through, about 10 minutes. Just before serving, stir in sour cream as desired. Serve ravioli on individual plates, top with pumpkin sauce, and sprinkle with Parmesan cheese.
- Servings: 6
- Nutritional Information Per Serving: Calories 240; Total fat 8g; Saturated fat 4g; Cholesterol 30mg; Sodium 520mg; Carbohydrate 36g; Fiber 6g; Protein 10g; Vitamin A 220%DV*; Vitamin C 6%DV; Calcium 15%DV; Iron 10%DV *Daily Value

10. Cheese Ravioli With Toasted Walnuts Recipe

Serving: 4 | Prep: | Cook: 15mins | Ready in:

Ingredients

- One 14- 16 ounce package cheese ravioli (I used the fresh ones)
- 1/3 cup olive oil
- 1 clove garlic sliced (I used two large cloves)
- 1 cup walnuts roughly chopped (I will decrease this next time)
- 2 teaspoons lemon juice
- 1/2 teaspoon kosher salt and 1/4 teaspoon pepper
- 1/2 cup flat leaf parsley chopped
- 1/4 cup parmesan

Direction

- Cook ravioli according to package,
- Drain and reserve 3 tablespoons of cooking water
- Meanwhile heat oil in skillet over medium heat.
- Add garlic and walnuts, cook stirring about 5 minutes until fragrant
- Stir in lemon juice, salt and pepper, parsley and cooking water
- Add ravioli and toss to coat
- Plate and sprinkle with Parmesan

11. Cheese Ravioli And Spinach Salad Recipe

Serving: 4 | Prep: | Cook: 10mins | Ready in:

Ingredients

- 10 ounce package fresh spinach rinsed and patted dry
- 25 ounce package frozen cheese ravioli cooked according to package directions

- 1 large red bell pepper cut in a few rings for garnish then the rest in bite size strips
- 2/3 cup balsamic vinaigrette
- 1 cup prepared chunky salsa
- pitted black olives for garnish

Direction

- Place spinach in a large shallow salad bowl and top with hot ravioli and sliced red pepper.
- Toss gently with vinaigrette and salsa being careful to not break up ravioli.
- Garnish with bell pepper rings and black olives.

12. Chevre And Spinach Wonton Ravioli With Fresh Parsley Sauce Recipe

Serving: 4 | Prep: | Cook: 10mins | Ready in:

Ingredients

- 6oz chevre, softened
- 1 3/4 cup ricotta
- 4-5 oz fresh spinach, chopped fine
- 6-8oz fresh mushrooms, chopped
- 2 green onions, greens only, chopped
- 2-3 cloves garlic, minced
- salt and pepper
- 2T olive oil
- sea or kosher salt and fresh ground pepper
- fresh grated nutmeg, optional, about 1/2t
- 1 package wonton wrappers(these would be better to use TWO wontons per ravioli as one is just too thin, as you can see in my photo :) Or, you can use the thicker "dumpling" wrappers that are sometimes available)
- Large pot of water brought to a boil, then reduced to high simmer
- parsley Sauce
- 1/2 cup fresh parsley, finely chopped
- 1/4-1/2 cup high quality olive oil
- 3 cloves garlic, crushed
- 1/4 cup fresh Parmesan, grated
- salt and pepper

Direction

- Heat 2T oil in medium skillet. Add mushrooms and garlic, then spinach, and cook about 5 minutes until mushrooms are just beginning to cook and spinach is cooked down but still bright green. (Don't overcook the spinach, it will turn bitter)
- Drain and let cool
- Meanwhile, combine cheeses, onion, salt, pepper and nutmeg in medium bowl.
- Add spinach/mushroom mixture and fold until combined.
- Spoon about 1T mixture into the center of each wonton wrapper
- With fingertip or small pastry brush, dampen edges with water
- Fold one corner to its opposite corner, pressing edges together to seal.
- Drop raviolis into simmering water, about 4-5 at a time and cook 5-8 minutes, till al dente or desired texture
- Remove with large slotted spoon and drain.
- Combine all ingredients for sauce other than oil, then whisk in oil just before serving.
- Serve raviolis with small amount of sauce over them.

13. Chicken Alfredo Ravioli Bake Recipe

Serving: 8 | Prep: | Cook: 60mins | Ready in:

Ingredients

- 2 tablespoons butter
- 1 1/4 pounds boneless skinless chicken breast halves, cut into 1-inch pieces
- 1 (8-ounce) package sliced fresh mushrooms
- 1 (16-ounce) jar alfredo sauce
- 1 (25 to 27 1/2-ounce) package frozen cheese-filled ravioli

- 1 large (1 cup) red bell pepper, chopped
- 8 ounces (2 cups) mozzarella cheese, shredded
- 1/4 cup shredded parmesan cheese

Direction

- Heat oven to 350°F. Melt butter in 12-inch skillet until sizzling; add chicken pieces. Cook over medium-high heat until chicken is lightly browned (4 to 6 minutes). Add mushrooms; continue cooking until chicken is no longer pink and mushrooms are tender (4 to 6 minutes). Do not drain.
- Spread 1/2 cup sauce into greased 13x9-inch baking dish. Arrange single layer of frozen ravioli over sauce; drizzle 3/4 cup sauce evenly over ravioli. Spread with 1 1/2 cups chicken and mushroom mixture, 1/2 cup red bell pepper and 1 cup mozzarella cheese. Repeat with remaining ingredients, except remaining 1 cup mozzarella cheese and Parmesan cheese. Cover tightly with aluminum foil. Bake for 45 minutes.
- Remove foil; sprinkle with remaining mozzarella and Parmesan cheese. Bake, uncovered, for 15 to 20 minutes or until cheeses are melted. Let stand 15 minutes before serving.
- Recipe Tip
- To make ahead, prepare as directed above except do not bake. Cover; refrigerate up to 24 hours. When ready to bake, continue as directed above. Increase first baking time to 1 hour.

14. Chicken Marsala Ravioli Recipe

Serving: 4 | Prep: | Cook: 15mins | Ready in:

Ingredients

- 24 each chicken ravioli, thawed not frozen
- 4 oz butter flavored Oil
- 8 oz Fresh sliced mushrooms
- 2 oz Smoked prosciutto, diced
- 4 oz asparagus, bias sliced
- 1 tsp sea salt
- black pepper to taste
- 24 oz heavy cream
- 4 oz marsala cooking wine
- 2 Tsp basil, julienned
- 2 oz parmesan cheese, grated
- 4 each basil sprigs (for garnish)

Direction

- Place chicken ravioli in boiling water for 2 ½ to 3 minutes.
- In a heated sauté pan, add butter flavored oil, mushrooms, smoked prosciutto, asparagus, sea salt, black pepper and sauté for about 30 seconds, or until mushrooms are cooked through.
- Add Marsala wine, heavy cream, julienned basil and simmer for about 2 to 4 minutes.
- Remove chicken ravioli from water and drain well.
- Add ravioli to sauté pan and toss until coated.
- Place ravioli on platter, pillow side up.
- Pour sauce evenly over ravioli.
- Garnish with fresh basil sprigs.

15. Chicken Amp Spinach Ravioli Recipe

Serving: 6 | Prep: | Cook: 30mins | Ready in:

Ingredients

- 4 eggs; beaten
- ¾ c water
- 3 ¾ c flour
- 1 ½ t salt
- ½ lb ground chicken
- ¾ c chopped spinach
- 2 T finely chopped onion
- 3 T melted butter
- 3 T grated asiago cheese

- ¼ t salt
- ¼ t garlic powder
- 1/8 t nutmeg
- ground pepper to taste
- 16 oz marinara sauce
- ¼ c grated Asiago for topping

Direction

- In mixing bowl, combine eggs, water, 2 c flour, salt. Gradually mix in remaining flour. Divide dough in 2 parts. Cover, refrigerate 20m.
- Cook ground chicken until evenly browned, drain. Mix chicken, spinach and onion in food processor. Mix chicken mixture with butter, 3 T cheese, salt, garlic, nutmeg and pepper.
- On a lightly floured surface, roll out each part of the dough to 1/8" thickness. Cut into 2" squares. Place about 1 t of chicken mixture in the center of ½ the squares and top with remaining squares. Seal the edges of the squares with a wet fork to form ravioli.
- Bring a large pot of lightly salted water to a boil and cook the ravioli in small batches for about 8 mins. Drain, rinse under cold water.
- Place the marinara sauce in a pan and cook until heated. Serve ravioli topped with marinara sauce and remaining cheese.

16. Chinese Dumplings Recipe

Serving: 2 | Prep: | Cook: |Ready in:

Ingredients

- for the dough
- 75g of flour
- 1/3 glass of water
- oil droplet
- for the filling
- 2 carrots
- 50g of savoy cabbage
- 2 zucchini
- 1 medium onion
- a pinch of sesame
- a few little slices of fresh ginger
- 1 tsp of olive oil

Direction

- Cut all the vegetables in thin slices, and put them all in a pan with oil. Cook for 15-20'
- Prepare the dough and let rest it for about 10' minutes, then spread it with a rolling pin.
- Remove the pan from the stove, and let it cold.
- Prepare a pot for steaming.
- Do with a large glass circles in the spreaded dough, and put in it a teaspoon of filling, close the crescent dough.
- Put the dumpling on the steaming pot, and let it cook for about 10'.
- Serve with a dash of soy sauce.

17. Crab And Smoked Salmon Ravioli Recipe

Serving: 8 | Prep: | Cook: 20mins |Ready in:

Ingredients

- 3 ounces skinless smoked salmon fillet
- 3 tablespoons chilled whipping cream
- 1 tablespoon egg white
- 4 ounces fresh crabmeat
- 1 green onion chopped
- 1/2 celery stalk finely diced
- 2 teaspoons chopped fresh cilantro
- 1-1/2 teaspoons fresh lemon juice
- 1/8 teaspoon salt
- 1/8 teaspoon freshly ground black pepper
- 32 potsticker wrappers
- Vinaigrette:
- 1 cup olive oil
- 1/4 cup white wine vinegar
- 1/4 cup fresh lemon juice
- 2 tomatoes peeled seeded and diced
- 3 ounces snow peas cut into strips
- 1 celery stalk cut into strips
- 3 tablespoons minced fresh chives

Direction

- Remove any bones from salmon then chop coarsely and transfer to food processor.
- Add cream and egg white then puree and transfer to boil.
- Mix in crab, onion, celery, cilantro, lemon juice, salt and pepper.
- Place 1 wrapper on work surface and put 1 level tablespoon filling in center.
- Brush edges with water then cover with another wrapper and press firmly to seal.
- Transfer to prepared sheet then repeat with remaining wrappers and filling.
- Cover with plastic and chill then bring large saucepan of water to a boil.
- Add wrappers in batches and cook until tender about 3 minutes per batch.
- Using slotted spoon transfer wrappers to another baking sheet then cover with foil.
- Combine oil, vinegar and lemon juice in large skillet then stir over medium heat until warm.
- Add tomatoes, snow peas and celery then stir just until heated through about 2 minutes.
- Add chives then divide mixture among plates and place ravioli on top of vinaigrette.

18. Crabmeat Ravioli Recipe

Serving: 5 | Prep: | Cook: 30mins | Ready in:

Ingredients

- 1/4 cup olive oil
- 1 yellow onion, small dice
- 1 summer squash, small dice
- 1 zucchini, smll dice
- 2 teaspoons mixed fresh herbs
- 1 pound lump crabmeat, remove all shells
- 1/2 cup Dried bread Crumbs
- 1 bunch green onions
- salt and white pepper to taste
- ***Ravioli Pasta:***
- 4 pounds semolina flour
- 1 pound all-purpose flour
- 1 tablespoon salt
- 6 eggs and enough water to total
- 16 ounces of liquid
- ***Lemon basil butter Sauce:***
- 1/4 cup white wine
- 1/4 cup seasoned rice vinegar
- 2 tablespoons lemon juice
- 1 Shallot, minced
- 1 pound Whole butter (cut into cubes)
- 1/8 cup heavy cream
- 2 tablespoons fresh basil (cut into strips)
- salt and pepper to taste

Direction

- Crabmeat Filling:
- Heat olive oil in sauce pan over medium-high heat. Add yellow onion and cook until translucent, about 5 minutes. Add squash and zucchini, cook 5-7 minutes. Add salt, white pepper, mixed herbs and green onions. Cook additional 5 minutes. Remove mixture from heat, pour into colander to drain all liquid. Once mixture has cooled, add crabmeat and bread crumbs. Season to taste.
- Ravioli Pasta:
- Combine all ingredients and use pasta maker, if no machine available roll out dough to desire thickness and cut into two even sheets. Lightly egg wash the bottom sheet and then place balls of filling 2 1/2 inches apart.
- Cover filling with the remaining sheet of pasta (do not egg wash) and cut into equal squares. Use your fingers to press edges together (removing any air pockets) and place on cornmeal dusted cookie sheet. Sprinkle ravioli with cornmeal and proceed to cooking instructions.
- To Cook Pasta: Place ravioli in boiled salted water and cook for 3 1/2 to 4 minutes, then drain. Add cooked ravioli to sauce as directed.
- Lemon Basil Butter Sauce:
- In a small sauce pan, combine white wine, rice vinegar, lemon juice and shallots. Over medium heat reduce until syrupy. Add cream and reduce by half. Adjust heat to low. Whisk

in one cube of butter at a time, making sure each cube of butter is melted before you add the next, until all the butter is incorporated. Strain and season with salt, pepper and basil. Toss cooked raviolis in sauce and serve immediately.

19. Crabmeat Ravioli With Clam Sauce Recipe

Serving: 6 | Prep: | Cook: 80mins | Ready in:

Ingredients

- Sauce:
- 1 tablespoon olive oil
- 1/3 cup finely chopped onion
- 2 garlic cloves, minced
- 1 (28-ounce) can crushed tomatoes, undrained
- 1 (14.5-ounce) can no-salt-added diced tomatoes
- 2 tablespoons chopped fresh flat-leaf parsley
- 1 tablespoon chopped fresh oregano
- 1/4 teaspoon salt
- 1/4 teaspoon crushed red pepper
- 1/4 teaspoon black pepper
- 1 (10-ounce) can clams, drained
- Ravioli:
- 1/2 pound lump crabmeat, drained and shell pieces removed
- 1/2 cup finely chopped red bell pepper
- 2 tablespoons panko (Japanese breadcrumbs)
- 1 tablespoon chopped fresh chives
- 1/8 teaspoon salt
- 1/2 cup part-skim ricotta
- 24 round wonton wrappers or gyoza skins

Direction

- To prepare sauce, heat olive oil in a Dutch oven over medium-high heat. Add onion, and sauté 3 minutes or until tender. Add garlic, and sauté 1 minute. Add crushed and diced tomatoes; bring to a boil. Reduce heat, and simmer 30 minutes. Add the parsley, oregano, 1/4 teaspoon salt, crushed red pepper, black pepper, and clams; simmer for 10 minutes. Remove from heat, and set aside.
- To prepare ravioli, combine crab, chopped red bell pepper, panko, chives, and 1/8 teaspoon salt in a medium bowl. Add ricotta; stir gently to combine. Working with 1 wonton wrapper at a time (cover remaining wrappers with a damp towel to keep them from drying), spoon about 1 tablespoon crab mixture into center of each wrapper. Moisten edges of wrapper with water. Fold in half, pinching edges together to seal and create a half-moon shape. Repeat procedure with remaining wonton wrappers and crab mixture.
- Fill a large Dutch oven with water; bring water to a boil. Add half of ravioli; cook 4 minutes or until done. Remove ravioli from pan with a slotted spoon; keep warm. Repeat procedure with remaining ravioli. Serve ravioli immediately with sauce.

20. Creamy Chicken N Roasted Garlic Ravioli Lasagna Two Ways Recipe

Serving: 6 | Prep: | Cook: 35mins | Ready in:

Ingredients

- 1 package (9 ounces) BUITONI® Refrigerated chicken & roasted garlic Ravioli prepared according to package directions
- This has a spectacular taste!
- 1 container (15 ounces) BUITONI® Refrigerated marinara sauce
- or your homemade sauce
- 1/4 cup BUITONI® Refrigerated Pesto with basil orhomemade pesto
- 2 medium baby bella or white button mushrooms sliced fairly thin
- 4 ounces sliced smoked provolone cheese cut into strips
- 9 whole large fresh basil leaves

Direction

- PREHEAT oven to 350° F. Grease 8 x 4-inch loaf pan.
- COMBINE prepared pasta, sauce and pesto in large bowl.
- LINE bottom of loaf pan with one-fourth of pasta mixture. Layer with one-third of mushrooms, one-third of cheese and 3 basil leaves. Repeat layers two times, ending with remaining pasta mixture on top.
- Cover tightly with foil.
- BAKE for 35 to 40 minutes or until heated through. Let cool for 10 minutes before serving.

21. Denny's Sausage And Ricotta Ravioli Recipe

Serving: 3 | Prep: | Cook: 2hours | Ready in:

Ingredients

- For the dough
- 2 cups A/P flour
- 3 large eggs
- water
- For the sauce
- 1 tablespoons olive oil
- 1 garlic clove, crushed
- 1 14.5 oz can tomato sauce
- 1 14.5 oz can diced tomatoes
- 1 4 oz can tomato paste
- 1 cup water
- 2 teaspoons balsamic vinegar
- 1 tablespoon sugar
- 1 tablespoon dried oregano
- 1 tablespoon dried marjoram
- 1 tablespoon dried basil
- 1 tablespoon italian seasoning
- 1/2 cup grated parmigiano reggiano cheese
- 1 cup fresh basil, chopped
- salt and fresh ground pepper
- For the filling
- 1 pound mild Italian sausage
- 1 tablespoon italian seasoning
- 1 teaspoon garlic powder
- 1 teaspoon onion powder
- 1 pint Ricotta

Direction

- Pasta Dough
- Pulse the flour in a food processor to break up clumps so that the flour evenly absorbs the eggs.
- Add the eggs and process until a rough dough forms, about 30 seconds.
- If the dough resembles small pebbles, the dough is too dry; add water, 1/2 teaspoon at a time, and process until the dough forms a rough ball. If the dough sticks to the sides of the work bowl, the dough is too wet; add flour, 1 tablespoon at a time, and process until the dough forms a rough ball.
- Finish kneading the dough (and any stray bits) by hand. Turn the dough ball and small bits out onto a dry work surface. Knead by hand until the dough is smooth and elastic, 1 to 2 minutes.
- Cover the dough with plastic wrap and set it aside for at least 15 minutes and up to 2 hours to allow the gluten in the dough to relax
- Pasta Sauce
- Over medium heat, heat oil in a saucepan until hot.
- Add all ingredients except basil and cheese.
- Salt and pepper to taste.
- Cover and bring to a boil.
- Lower heat and allow to simmer for 45 minutes with the lid opened slightly.
- Stir the basil and parmesan into the sauce and season with salt and pepper.
- For a smoother sauce, blend with an immersion blender.
- For Ravioli, you will need to blend the sauce until smooth
- Filling
- Remove sausage from casings and brown in sauté pan
- Add seasonings while browning the meat

- Drain excess grease from meat and cool
- Once the meat is cool, add it to food processor along with ricotta cheese and pulse to break up meat and blend.

22. Easy Baked Ravioli Recipe

Serving: 4 | Prep: | Cook: 25mins | Ready in:

Ingredients

- 2 tsp. Zesty Italian dressing
- 1 medium red pepper, chopped
- 1 small onion, chopped
- 1 can (19 fl oz/540 mL) pasta sauce
- 1/4 tsp. crushed red pepper (optional)
- 1 pkg. (350 g) ravioli, cooked, drained
- 1/2 cup Part Skim Mozzarella Shredded cheese

Direction

- PREHEAT oven to 350°F.
- Heat dressing in large skillet on medium heat; add peppers and onions. Cook and stir 2 min. or until vegetables are crisp-tender.
- Stir in pasta sauce and crushed red pepper.
- SPREAD 1/2 cup of the sauce mixture onto bottom of shallow 11x7-inch baking dish.
- COVER with layers of half each of the ravioli, remaining sauce mixture and cheese. Repeat layers.
- Cover with foil.
- Bake 25 min. or until heated through.

23. Easy Homemade Ravioli Recipe

Serving: 4 | Prep: | Cook: 15mins | Ready in:

Ingredients

- 9 oz. ground round
- 3/4 lb. soft-style cream cheese
- 30 wonton wrappers
- 2-1/4 cups prepared spaghetti sauce
- 1 egg

Direction

- In a bowl stir together ground round and cream cheese.
- Place a spoonful of filling in the center of each wrapper.
- Brush wrapper edges with water or a beaten egg.
- Fold corner to corner to form triangle shape and press edges together firmly.
- Let lay for about 5 minutes to make sure they seal.
- Drop into boiling water and cook for 3-5 minutes or until meat is done.
- Heat sauce in a separate saucepan.
- Top ravioli with sauce.
- Try stuffing with minced pepperoni and cheeses... Yummy
- Enjoy!

24. Easy Ravioli No Need For A Pasta Machine Recipe

Serving: 4 | Prep: | Cook: 1hours | Ready in:

Ingredients

- For the pasta
- 10 ounces (250 grams) pasta flour
- 3 eggs, beaten
- 1 tablespoon olive oil
- For the spinach and ricotta filling
- A handful of baby spinach leaves
- 4 ounces (100 grams) ricotta cheese
- A handful of grated parmesan
- salt and pepper
- For the bean pate filling
- 8 ounces (200 grams) of fresh broad beans in their pods, shelled to give about 4 ounces
- 4 ounces (100 grams) goats cheese

- 1 garlic clove, crushed
- 1 tablespoon lemon juice
- 1 tablespoon olive oil
- salt and pepper

Direction

- For the pasta
- Simply place the flour on a clean surface and make a well in the middle.
- Pour in the beaten eggs and slowly combine.
- Add the oil as required to form a firm ball of dough, and knead until smooth.
- Wrap the dough in Clingfilm and rest whilst you make the filling.
- For the spinach and ricotta filling
- Place all ingredients in a bowl and mash together with a fork, adding a little olive oil if needed.
- For the bean pate filling
- Cook the broad beans in boiling water for 8-10 minutes until tender. Push them out of their skins, and place in a food processor.
- Blend the beans with the remaining ingredients.
- To make the ravioli
- Roll out the dough on a floured surface as thin as it will go (a millimetre or two).
- Use a round cutter (3-4 inches diameter) to cut out pasta shapes. Keep the pasta rounds under a damp tea towel to prevent them drying out before use.
- Using a teaspoon, place your desired filling on a round, brush the edges of the pasta with water, and stick another round on top. Repeat until you have used up all your pasta!
- Cook in boiling water for 4-8 minutes, depending on the thickness of your pasta and serve with a drizzle of extra virgin olive oil.

25. Easy Ravioli Bake Recipe

Serving: 8 | Prep: | Cook: 70mins | Ready in:

Ingredients

- 1 jar (26 to 28 oz.) tomato pasta sauce
- 1 pkg. 25 to 27-1/2 oz) frozen cheese filled ravioli or any kind of meat filled ravioli
- 2 cups shredded mozzarella cheese
- 2 Tbsp. grated parmesan cheese

Direction

- Heat oven to 350*F.
- Spray bottom and sides of a 13x9x2" baking dish with cooking spray.
- Spread 3/4 cup of the pasta sauce in baking dish.
- Arrange half the frozen ravioli in a single layer.
- Top with half of the remaining pasta sauce and 1 cup of the mozzarella cheese.
- Repeat layers once, starting with ravioli.
- Sprinkle with Parmesan cheese.
- Cover with foil and bake 40 minutes.
- Remove foil baked 20 minutes longer until bubbly and hot.
- Let stand 10 minutes before cutting

26. Easy Ravioli Casserole Recipe

Serving: 8 | Prep: | Cook: 30mins | Ready in:

Ingredients

- 1 32oz can of beef ravioli
- 1 jar or can of pasta sauce
- 1lb of italian flavored turkey (can substitute 1lb of ground beef and season to taste)
- 8 oz shredded mozzerella cheese

Direction

- Preheat oven to 350 degrees
- Brown turkey in skillet until done
- Rinse sauce from canned ravioli until pasta is clean
- Spray non-stick cooking spray on bottom and sides of 13x9 dish

- Spread thin layer of pasta sauce, just enough to coat entire bottom of dish
- Place single layer of ravioli in bottom of dish
- Sprinkle 1/2 of browned meat on top of ravioli
- Gently spread sauce over meat and ravioli
- Top with 1/2 shredded cheese
- Repeat process until pan is full and/or ingredients gone
- Bake approximately 20 minutes or until cheese is melted and beginning to brown
- Let cool for approximately 3 minutes
- Serve
- For less spicy meat use ground beef and season to taste or mix Italian turkey and ground beef together

- Blanch the tomatoes in a pot of rapidly boiling water for 20 seconds, then plunge into a pot of cold water to stop the cooking.
- Peel, seed, and chop the tomatoes into a small dice.
- Add diced tomatoes to the garlic and onion along with the basil.
- Cook for about 15 minutes at low-to-medium heat, stirring occasionally.
- Add the eggplant and cook until the mixture reaches the consistency of a thick paste.
- Mix in the goat cheese.
- Let the mixture cool and put a small spoonful onto each square of pasta dough. You can also use a pastry bag, which gives you far more control over the amount of filling you dispense.

27. Eggplant Ravioli Filling Recipe

Serving: 4 | Prep: | Cook: 20mins | Ready in:

Ingredients

- 1 lb. eggplant
- salt
- 1 tsp butter
- 1 tsp olive oil
- 2 cloves garlic, finely chopped
- 1 small onion, finely chopped
- 2 ripe roma tomatoes
- 8 basil leaves
- ¼ cup goat cheese

Direction

- Peel and slice the eggplant, sprinkle with salt, and place in a colander.
- Leave for 1 hour to draw out the bitter juices. Rinse and dry.
- Finely chop and set aside.
- Heat the butter and oil over medium heat in a medium-sized saucepan.
- Add the garlic and onion and sauté gently for a few minutes. Don't let the garlic burn.

28. Elaines Homemade Beef N Cheese Ravioli Recipe

Serving: 4 | Prep: | Cook: 90mins | Ready in:

Ingredients

- 2 lbs lean ground beef
- 1 can diced tomatoes, large size
- 3 oz dry red wine
- grated OLD cheese (amount to your preference)
- 3 tbsp dehydrated onion
- 4 green onions, coarsely chopped
- 1 ½ tsp basil
- 1 ½ tsp garlic powder (NOT garlic salt!)
- parsley to taste (added at the end of cooking time)
- 4 eggs
- ½ cup cold water
- 3 ½ cups best-for-bread flour

Direction

- For the pasta:
- In a bowl, place the flour and the eggs
- Stir with a fork to combine

- Add the water
- Continue mixing until all is well combined
- Knead gently for about 5 minutes, then allow the dough to rest for ten, covered, so it doesn't dry out
- After the resting period, break off fist-sized pieces of the pasta dough
- Keeping it well floured, roll the piece between the palms of your hands
- Next, place the chunk on the pasta machine (I use a hand-crank, because I find it gives the best control) on setting no. 1
- Pass it through.
- Turn the control knob to 2nd position, and pass the dough strip through again.
- Continue increasing the pressure size until the pasta strip is about 1/8th of an inch thick
- Now it's ready for you to add the filling.
- ====================================
  =====
- The ravioli prep:
- Break the meat (see under 'the filling') into small enough bite-size pieces to fit on the pasta, as illustrated in the pics provided.
- Top each bite with grated old cheese.
- Don't overcrowd, or it will not seal and cut properly!
- Either fold over the other half of the pasta strip, OR make 2 strips, and set one on top of the other.
- Press down in between each bite to mark where you will cut with the cookie cutter.
- Press with the cookie cutter to bind both edges.
- Press and TWIST at the same time to ensure an even cut is made.
- Place the ravioli shapes on a plate, and allow to air-dry.
- Turn them over to dry the undersides after 1/2 hour or so.
- Leave air-drying until you're ready to cook them.
- The drier they are, the better…
- ====================================
  =====
- The filling:

- Start with 2 slices of bacon in a saucepan.
- When cooked, break up into pieces.
- Add the ground beef.
- Add the dried onion
- Add the garlic powder
- Add salt to your preference of taste
- Simmer until the meat is cooked; turn off the heat.
- ====================================
  =====
- The sauce:
- To the remaining meat in the pan, add the can of tomatoes and 1 cup of cold water.
- Add salt to your taste preference.
- Add the green onions
- Add the dry red wine
- Simmer over low flame until the sauce begins to reduce
- ====================================
  =====
- To cook the ravioli:
- Add the ravioli directly to the sauce, and simmer until the pasta is tender.
- Cover with a lid to steam the pasta thoroughly.
- ====================================
  =====
- NOTES:
- This is a very EASY dish, even though it might sound complicated.
- The only tricky part is in making the pasta.
- I've made pasta from 'scratch' for years, and it DOES take practice.
- So don't be too critical of yourself if you make it for the first few times, and it doesn't work out!!!
- If I can help walk you through it, PLEASE don't hesitate to give me a shout.
- It is really not as hard to make as you might think.
- One word of advice --- don't attempt to make pasta on a humid day.
- The humidity will not permit the gluten in the flour to work as well.
- Have fun with this recipe.
- It's ALL homemade, and delicious.

- HAPPY COOKING!

29. Feta Cheese Ravioli With Yellow Pepper Sauce Recipe

Serving: 4 | Prep: | Cook: 10mins | Ready in:

Ingredients

- For the pepper sauce
- 2 yellow peppers cut in pieces
- 1 onion chopped
- 50 ml cream
- 2 tbs olive oil
- 1/4 tsp salt
- For the filling
- 200 gr feta cheese or other sheep cheese
- 200 gr katiki cheese or other creamy cheese like ricotta or philadelfia
- 2 egg yolks
- 1/2 tsp grated nutmeg
- 1 bunch peppermint chopped
- For the ravioli dough
- 300 gr flour
- 3 eggs
- For garnish
- 1 red bell pepper

Direction

- Prepare the ravioli dough mixing the flour and eggs, then form a ball, cover it with plastic wrap and leave in the fridge for 1 hour.
- In a double-boiler melt the feta and katiki cheese and add the rest of the ingredients.
- Roll out the dough into two sheets of similar size.
- Place small balls of the filling onto the one sheet and cover with the other. Cut into traditional ravioli squares using a pastry cutter.
- Boil in plenty of salted water for 4 minutes.
- Prepare the sauce, sautéing the onion in the olive oil.
- Add the pepper pieces, salt and 2 tbsp. of water and cook until soft.
- Puree in the blender, strain and add the cream.
- Cook again until our mixture is creamy and smooth and set aside keeping it warm.
- Cut the red pepper in thin long strips.
- Sauté the ravioli and the red pepper for 1-2 minutes in butter.
- Serve with some sauce on a plate with the ravioli on top and decorate with some red pepper strips.

30. Fiesta Ravioli Recipe

Serving: 4 | Prep: | Cook: 15mins | Ready in:

Ingredients

- 1 package (25 ounces) frozen beef ravioli
- 1 can (10 ounces) enchilada sauce
- 1 jar (8 ounces) salsa
- 2 cups (8 ounces) shredded monterey jack cheese
- 1 can (2-1/4 ounces) sliced ripe olives, drained

Direction

- Cook ravioli according to package directions.
- Meanwhile, in a large skillet, combine enchilada sauce and salsa. Cook and stir over medium heat until heated through.
- Drain ravioli; add to sauce and gently toss to coat.
- Top with cheese and olives.
- Cover and cook over low heat for 3-4 minutes or until cheese is melted.

31. Foie Gras Ravioli With Port Currant Reduction Recipe

Serving: 4 | Prep: | Cook: 1hours30mins | Ready in:

Ingredients

- Homemade pasta sheets (or won ton wrappers)
- ~
- Filling:
- 1/2 cup zante currants (divided), soaked in port wine
- 1 tablespoon butter
- 1/4 cup onion, minced
- 6 oz fresh foie gras, chopped
- 1 (about 6 oz) pork chop
- 2 chicken leg thigh pieces
- a few sprigs of fresh thyme
- 1 organic egg
- kosher salt, white pepper, nutmeg - to taste
- white truffle butter, to finish (you can use truffle oil and regular butter instead)
- Sauce:
- reserved port from soaked currants
- 1/2 cup balsamic vinegar
- 1/4 cup soaked zante currants

Direction

- For port-currant reduction:
- Soak currants in enough port to just cover them for 1-2 hours. Reserve 1/4 cup for filling. In a small sauce pan, pour in the other 1/4 cup of soaked currants along with the port they soaked in. Add balsamic and slowly reduce until it just starts to become syrupy 9it also thickens as it cools so be careful not to over reduce). Set aside.
- For filling:
- Preheat oven to 350 degrees. Season chicken with salt and pepper. Place in baking dish along with fresh thyme and roast for about 45 minutes, or until deep golden brown and skin is crispy. Let cool.
- Turn up oven temp to broil. Season pork chop the same as the chicken and broil for about 8 minutes (do not overcook!) Let cool.
- Sauté onion in butter until soft; set aside.
- Remove meat from chicken, coarsely chop pork chop and place both in food processor. Add sautéed onion and foie gras. Pulse until almost smooth (you still want a little texture in there). Add egg and pulse a few more times to incorporate. Transfer to bowl, add remaining 1/4 cup soaked currants and season to taste . Note: If mixture is too wet, just add a little cornstarch.
- Fill fresh pasta dough (or wonton wrappers) with filling . Seal and cut . Bring a large pot of water to a boil and cook ravioli until they float to the top.
- Melt truffle butter in a large sauté pan and add drained ravioli. Transfer to serving plate and drizzle around the port-currant reduction. You can top the ravioli with fresh thyme leaves, if desired.

32. Fresh English Pea Ravioli With Salsa Verde Recipe

Serving: 6 | Prep: | Cook: 3mins | Ready in:

Ingredients

- 1 recipe of fresh pasta dough (link to my recipe below):
- semolina-pasta.html">Fresh Semolina Pasta
- ~~~~~~
- For Ravioli:
- 2 cups fresh English peas, podded
- 1 tablespoon unsalted butter
- 1 shallot, minced
- 2 tablespoons marscarpone cheese
- 2 tablespoons freshly grated parmigiano-reggiano
- 1 teaspoon fresh thyme leaves
- white pepper and kosher salt, to taste
- pinch of nutmeg
- ~~~~~~
- Salsa Verde:
- 1/2 cup each tightly packed fresh basil, Italian parsley, and mint
- 1 cups extra-virgin olive oil

- 1/4 cup red wine vinegar
- 1 tablespoon capers
- 1 garlic clove
- pinch of salt

Direction

- For salsa verde: In blender or food processor, purée all ingredients until smooth. Store in an airtight container until ready to use.
- Steam peas until tender (I set aside a few peas for garnish). Add peas to food processor. Sprinkle with a little salt and white pepper.
- Melt butter in sauté pan and add the shallots. Gently cook until soft. Add to peas.
- Add mascarpone, parmesan, nutmeg and thyme and pulse until smooth. Taste for seasoning and add more salt/pepper if needed. Transfer filling to small bowl.
- Bring a pot of water to a boil. Divide the pasta dough in half and roll each into thin sheets for ravioli. Lay the pasta sheets on a lightly floured board and lightly brush with water.
- Place approximately two tablespoons of the filling about two inches from each other. Place a second sheet over the first and push down gently around the filling, making sure that all of the edges are sealed and there isn't any air trapped inside.
- Use a large round cookie cutter, to cut each ravioli.
- Cook ravioli in the boiling water, about 3 minutes, until al dente. When they float to the top that is a sign they are ready. With a slotted spoon transfer ravioli into a shallow bowl. Add a few tablespoons of the salsa verde and gently toss to coat.
- To serve, drizzle a little salsa verde on the plate and place raviolis on top. Sprinkle with shaved parmesan and additional peas, if using. A fresh sprig of basil or mint would be nice too :-)

33. Fried Ravioli Recipe

Serving: 4 | Prep: | Cook: 15mins | Ready in:

Ingredients

- vegetable oil, for frying
- 1 large egg
- 2 Tbsp. milk
- 2/3 cups seasoned bread crumbs
- 24 refrigerated cheese ravioli
- 1/4 cup grated parmesan cheese
- 2 cups jarred marinara sauce

Direction

- Pour enough vegetable oil into a large, deep pot so that it reaches a depth of 1 inch. Warm oil over medium heat until a deep-fry thermometer registers 325F. Line a baking sheet with parchment or foil, and line a plate with paper towels.
- While vegetable oil is heating, whisk together egg and milk in a shallow bowl. Place bread crumbs in a separate shallow bowl.
- Working in batches, dip ravioli into egg mixture, allowing excess to drip back into bowl, then coat with bread crumbs. Place coated ravioli on baking sheet. Discard any remaining bread crumbs.
- Fry ravioli in batches, turning occasionally, until golden brown, about 3 minutes total. Be careful not to crowd ravioli in pan, and make sure oil comes back to 325F before adding another batch of ravioli.
- Transfer fried ravioli to lined plate to drain. Sprinkle fried ravioli with grated Parmesan cheese.
- Warm marinara sauce in a pan over medium-low heat or in a microwave. Spoon sauce into 4 small bowls.
- Serve fried ravioli with warmed marinara on the side.

34. Gluten Free Cheese Raviolis Recipe

Serving: 12 | Prep: | Cook: 5mins | Ready in:

Ingredients

- 1 cup Garfava flour
- 1/2 teaspoon salt
- 2 eggs
- 2 teaspoons Xantham Gum
- 2 teaspoons olive oil
- cornstarch
- FILLING
- 1 8oz container of Ricotta
- A pinch of white pepper(optional)
- 1 teaspoon dried parsley
- 2 Tablespoons grated romano cheese
- 1 egg

Direction

- . Place the flour, salt, xanthan gum, eggs and olive oil into a large bowl mix all together.
- . Form a dough ball
- .Cut the ball in half and cover with a damp cloth
- Put the dough onto a board and sprinkle with cornstarch
- .Knead the dough in the cornstarch
- Roll the dough out as thin as you can (this takes muscles)
- . Use a square or round cookie cutter and cut out 12 pieces
- . Put 1 Tablespoon of the filling on each square
- . Repeat # 4 5 6 7 and 8 and then crimp the edges on both sides with a folk.
- 10. Cook in boiling water for about 5 minutes. Add your favorite sauce. I place them on a cookie sheet in the freezer. They freeze very well!

35. Gorgonzola Cream Sauce

Serving: 0 | Prep: | Cook: |Ready in:

Ingredients

- 1 cup heavy whipping cream
- salt and freshly ground black pepper to taste
- 1 pinch cayenne pepper, or to taste
- 6 ounces dry miniature ravioli
- 3 ounces crumbled Gorgonzola cheese
- 2 tablespoons chopped Italian flat leaf parsley
- 2 tablespoons freshly grated Parmesan cheese
- ½ apple, diced
- ¼ cup chopped toasted walnuts
- 1 teaspoon chopped Italian flat leaf parsley

Direction

- Place a heavy skillet over medium heat. Pour cream into skillet, bring to a simmer, and cook cream until it reduces by half, about 8 minutes, stirring occasionally. Season with salt, black pepper, and cayenne pepper.
- Bring a pot of salted water to a boil. Pour dried ravioli into boiling water and cook, stirring occasionally, until pasta is tender, 16 to 18 minutes. Drain pasta, reserving a cup of pasta water.
- Gently fold cooked ravioli into cream sauce and turn heat to low. Mix in Gorgonzola cheese, stirring gently until melted. If sauce is too thick, thin it with a little pasta cooking water.
- Stir in 2 tablespoons parsley and Parmesan cheese. Transfer to a serving bowl and sprinkle with diced apple, walnuts, and 1 teaspoon parsley.
- Nutrition Facts
- Per Serving:
- 299.7 calories; protein 8.5g 17% DV; carbohydrates 12.6g 4% DV; fat 24.4g 38% DV; cholesterol 81.8mg 27% DV; sodium 257.7mg 10% DV.

36. Grammys Raviolis Recipe

Serving: 12 | Prep: | Cook: 4mins | Ready in:

Ingredients

- 1 cup Garfava flour
- 1/2 teaspoon salt
- 2 eggs
- 2 teaspoons Xantham gum
- 2 teaspoons olive oil
- cornstarch
- Filling
- 1 egg
- 2 Tablespoons of romano cheese
- 1 tsp dried parley
- a pinch of white pepper
- 1 8oz ricotta cheese(low fat if you wish)

Direction

- In a large bowl add flour, salt, olive oil, xanthan gum and eggs
- Mix together until you are able to form a ball
- Cut the ball in half and cover the remainder with a wet cloth to keep it moist. Place the dough on a very firm board. Sprinkle the board with cornstarch. Knead the dough in the cornstarch. Roll the dough into a thin sheet (This is NOT easy) Use a round or square cookie cutter and cut out 12 Place about 1 tbsp. of the filling on the dough Repeat the same for the covering of the Ravioli. Crimp the edges with a folk on both sides to seal them. Cook in boiling water for about 4 or 5 minutes. Sometimes I make a double recipe. I have frozen the squares on a cookie sheet and just defrost and add the filling that works perfectly also.

37. Greek Style Beef And Cheese Ravioli Recipe

Serving: 4 | Prep: | Cook: 20mins | Ready in:

Ingredients

- 9 ounce package refrigerated cheese ravioli
- 1-1/4 pounds lean ground beef
- 2 cans diced tomatoes with basil, garlic and oregano with juice
- 2 cups lightly packed fresh baby spinach plus additional leaves for garnish
- 1 cup pitted ripe olives
- 3/4 cup crumbled feta cheese

Direction

- Cook ravioli according to package directions then drain.
- Meanwhile brown ground beef in deep non-stick skillet over medium heat for 6 minutes.
- Stir in tomatoes then bring to a boil and reduce heat and simmer 10 minutes.
- Stir in ravioli then simmer 3 minutes and stir in spinach and olives.
- Cook just until spinach is wilted then sprinkle with cheese before serving.
- Garnish with fresh spinach leaves and serve immediately.

38. Ham And Leek Ravioli Recipe

Serving: 4 | Prep: | Cook: 30mins | Ready in:

Ingredients

- 1 leek white part only thinly sliced
- 1 tablespoon butter
- 1/2 tablespoon heavy cream
- 2 ounces ham finely diced
- 1 teaspoon freshly ground black pepper
- 24 round wonton skins
- 1 egg beaten

Direction

- Cook leek in the butter in a small sauté pan over medium heat for 5 minutes
- Add cream and cook for 2 minutes longer then set aside to cool

- In a bowl combine leek with ham and season with pepper
- Lay 12 wonton skins on flat surface and place spoonful of ham mixture in center of each wonton
- Brush edges of remaining 12 wonton skins with the egg and place over filling egg side down
- Firmly press edges of each ravioli together removing any air pockets and completely sealing
- Cook ravioli in boiling salted water for 4 minutes
- Remove ravioli from water with a slotted spoon and drain thoroughly in a colander

39. Hearty Ravioli Recipe

Serving: 4 | Prep: | Cook: 30mins | Ready in:

Ingredients

- 450 grams of spinach, large stems removed and chopped
- 1 tbs. grainy mustard
- 1 teaspoon sesame oil
- 1/2 teaspoon nutmeg
- 2 tbs. bread crumbs
- 1 c. semolina four
- 2 tsp. olive oil
- 1/2 cup water
- 1 can crushed tomatoes
- 1 onion, minced
- 1 tbs. olive oil
- 1 clove garlic, minced
- various Italian herbs (fresh would be best)
- salt and pepper to taste
- dash of lemon
- pinch of cayenne pepper

Direction

- In a bowl, combine the semolina flour, 2 tsp. olive oil, 1/2 cup water and a pinch salt to make a dough.
- Wrap in a towel and let sit for 30 minutes.
- Wash the spinach and remove the large tough stems.
- Chop the spinach and steam or sauté in water. (Sweat)
- Place in a large mixing bowl.
- Add the mustard, a pinch of salt and breadcrumbs and mix well.
- Season further with salt, cayenne and pepper.
- Set filling aside
- Sauté the minced onion in the olive oil until the onion is glassy.
- Add the minced garlic and sauté.
- Add the tomatoes and reduce heat to simmer.
- Add the herbs, lemon juice, salt and pepper and continue to simmer on a low heat.
- Season to taste with additional salt, pepper and cayenne.
- Set the sauce aside.
- Divide the dough in fourths and roll out each portion on a floured work space, allowing the first sheet of pasta to sit while rolling out the second. One of the tricks to the pasta is, to make sure you've rolled the dough out very thin (but not too thin!).
- Cut out your ravioli shapes and fill with the filling. Place the top part of the ravioli over the filling and close with a fork. If you have a form or press, then of course that saves time you merely place 1 sheet of dough on one side, put the filling on the dough and then lay the 2nd sheet of dough on top. Close the form to seal and cut off the extra using a knife.
- Meanwhile, bring a large pot of salty water to boil.
- Put your ravioli into the salty water and cook a few at a time. They are ready when they come floating to the top.
- Place the first cooked raviolis in the oven to keep warm until they are all ready.
- When ready to serve, put a layer of sauce on the plate and lay the raviolis on top.
- You can garnish with some fresh cut herbs or if you have soy cheese, you can dust some on top.

40. Homemade Mushroom And Ricotta Ravioli Recipe

Serving: 5 | Prep: | Cook: 5mins | Ready in:

Ingredients

- Dough:
- 2 1/2 cps flour
- 1 cp very hot water
- Filling:
- 3/4 cp ricotta
- 1 egg
- 1/2 cp mushrooms
- basil, salt & pepper to taste

Direction

- Combine flour and water in a mixing bowl.
- Stir and cover for 10 mins.
- Roll out dough and place teaspoonfuls of filling along it.
- Fold and seal.
- Boil 3 - 4 minutes.
- Serve as appetizer or main course and enjoy!

41. In Side Out Ravioli Recipe

Serving: 8 | Prep: | Cook: 30mins | Ready in:

Ingredients

- 1 lb. ground beef
- 1/2 cup onion, chopped
- 2 tbsp garlic, minced
- 1 tbsp italian seasoning
- 10-oz. package frozen spinach, chopped
- 1-lb. spaghetti sauce with mushrooms
- 8-oz. tomato sauce
- 6-oz. tomato paste
- 1/2 tsp. salt
- Dash of black pepper
- 7-oz. package Shell or elbow macaroni, cooked
- 2 cup sharp cheddar cheese, grated
- 1/2 cup Soft bread Crumbs
- 2 whole eggs, well-beaten
- 1/4 cup vegetable or salad oil

Direction

- Brown ground beef, chopped onion, minced garlic and Italian seasoning in a large skillet over medium heat. Drain excess fat, if necessary, and reserve.
- Cook chopped spinach as directed on the package; drain, and reserve the liquid. Add enough water to the reserved spinach water to make 1 cup. Combine spinach liquid with the spaghetti sauce, tomato sauce, tomato paste, and salt and pepper, and add to the browned meat and vegetables. Simmer for about 10 minutes to thoroughly combine meat with the sauces.
- Meanwhile, cook the elbow or shell macaroni as directed on the package, drain, and reserve. Combine the cooked spinach with the macaroni in a large mixing bowl. Add cheese, bread crumbs, eggs, and oil to the spinach and macaroni, stirring from the bottom to combine all ingredients.
- Spread the macaroni mixture into a 9-inch by 13-inch oven-proof baking dish.
- Cover with the meat sauce, and bake in a pre-heated 350-F degree oven for about a half an hour.
- This hearty one-dish meal goes perfectly with a leafy green salad and garlic toast.

42. Inside Out Ravioli Recipe

Serving: 6 | Prep: | Cook: 40mins | Ready in:

Ingredients

- 1 pound extra lean ground beef
- 1 medium white onion chopped
- 3 cloves garlic minced
- 16 ounces tomato sauce

- 6 ounces tomato paste
- 1 tablespoon dried parsley
- 1/2 teaspoon dried oregano
- 1/2 teaspoon salt
- 1/2 teaspoon freshly ground black pepper
- 6 ounces rigatoni pasta uncooked
- 10 ounces frozen spinach chopped
- 1 cup shredded cheddar cheese
- 1/2 cup soft bread crumbs
- 2 medium eggs beaten
- 1/4 cup grated parmesan cheese

Direction

- Brown ground beef, garlic and onion in a large skillet then drain off excess fat.
- Add tomato sauce, tomato paste, parsley, oregano, salt and pepper then simmer 10 minutes.
- Cook pasta according to package directions until just softened but not quite done.
- Drain and rinse with cold water then put back into pan in which it was cooked.
- Add cooked spinach, cheddar cheese, bread crumbs, eggs and parmesan.
- Spread mixture into greased rectangular baking pan then top with meat mixture.
- Sprinkle more parmesan on top then bake at 350 for 30 minutes.

43. Italian Pork Ravioli Filling Recipe

Serving: 8 | Prep: | Cook: 30mins | Ready in:

Ingredients

- ½ pound pork shoulder, trimmed of fat and cut into small chunks
- ¼ pound skinless, boneless chicken breast
- 2 ounces prosciutto, cut into small pieces
- 2 ounces mortadella sausage, casing removed
- 2 ounces grated fresh Parmesan
- A pinch of nutmeg
- 1 egg, beaten
- 1 shallot, finely minced
- 1 garlic clove, finely minced

Direction

- Grind the pork shoulder, chicken breast, prosciutto, and sausage in a food processor until the mixture resembles coarse, grey sand.
- Sauté the shallot and garlic in some olive oil until they are limp. Add the ground meat and continue cooking at low heat, stirring constantly, for about 20 minutes, until the mixture is fully cooked and reduced.
- Allow to filling to cool, then mix in the beaten egg, Parmesan, and nutmeg. Make certain the filling is completely blended, then cover the bowl and refrigerate for at least half an hour.
- Use the filling for your ravioli. Everyone probably has his or her own pasta recipe; mine consists of 2 cups semolina, 1 Tbsp. of olive oil, two eggs, one egg yolk, and a tsp. of kosher salt. I mix the semolina and salt thoroughly, then place the dry mixture in a large bowl, forming a well in the center. I put the eggs and olive oil in the well and begin incorporating the semolina and salt into the wet ingredients with a fork, starting from the center and working outward toward the edge of the circle. You can do this on a floured surface, but I like to use a large steel mixing bowl. Once I have a sticky dough, I place it in a stand mixture and knead it at medium speed, using the dough hook, for at least 7 or 8 minutes. Then I form the dough into a log about 8 inches long and 2 inches in diameter, wrapping it in plastic, and refrigerating it for a minimum of half an hour before feeding portions of it through my pasta maker.
- Once you've made this, you might want to vary the proportions of the various meats. It's really a matter of taste.
- By the way, this ravioli freezes extremely well. I put the individual raviolis into a Ziploc freezer bag, apportioning just enough in each bag for a couple of servings. The important thing is not to let them dry out before freezing.

To serve, just bring a pot of heavily salted water to a rolling boil, drop the raviolis one at a time into the water, and let them cook for about two or three minutes. You don't need to overcook them, since the filling is already cooked and the pasta should cook almost immediately after it's thawed.

44. Kathleens Sage Brown Butter Ravioli Recipe

Serving: 4 | Prep: | Cook: 10mins | Ready in:

Ingredients

- 1 stick of unsalted butter
- 1 cup of fresh sage leaves (chiffonade)
- 1 tsp sea salt
- 1 pkg fresh or frozen cheese ravioli
- Fresh grated parmesan cheese for topping.

Direction

- Boil ravioli according to package directions.
- After you drop ravioli, heat a skillet to medium high heat.
- Add one stick of butter and melt slowly.
- Turn heat up to high and add in sage leaves (they will spatter in the hot butter).
- Butter will foam lightly and as foam subsides, the butter will turn a nutty brown, and the sage leaves will become crispy. (Do not leave the butter unattended over heat as it will burn)
- Remove from heat and add salt.
- Drain ravioli and add to brown butter sauce to coat.
- Top with freshly grated Parmesan cheese.

45. Leftover Ravioli Recipe

Serving: 4 | Prep: | Cook: 30mins | Ready in:

Ingredients

- 3 cups leftover casserole or hot dish
- 20 won ton wrappers
- 1 jar favorite red or white sauce
- 1/2 cup grated parmesan cheese or similar

Direction

- Using an immersion blender or food processor or perhaps just a blender, puree leftovers until smooth or at least uniform smallness.
- Wet two sides of won ton wrapper
- Place teaspoon or scantly larger amount of puree in center of won ton. (This is a great opportunity to use that won ton press you were given at some point in time.)
- Seal won ton wrapper and repeat until done.
- Boil four to eight quarts of salted water to rolling boil status.
- Heat sauce in large sauté` pan or similar.
- Boil in batches leftover raviolis. We usually do four to six at time so as not to crowd them causing the ravioli to stick to each other.
- Drain with spider tool and simmer in sauce until ready to serve.
- Top with parmesan.

46. Lobster Ravioli With Mascarpone Cream Sauce Recipe

Serving: 2 | Prep: | Cook: 30mins | Ready in:

Ingredients

- 1 pkg. store bought lobster ravioli
- 1 cup mascarpone cheese
- 4 Tbl. butter
- 1/2 cup grated parmesan cheese
- 1/4 tsp. fresh grated nutmeg
- salt and white pepper, to taste
- heavy cream as needed

Direction

- Prepare ravioli according to package instructions.
- While ravioli cooks...
- Melt butter in a sauce pan over low heat.
- Add the mascarpone to the melted butter and stir until it has melted and combined.
- Add nutmeg to the mascarpone mixture and stir to combine.
- Add all of the Parmesan cheese at once and stir it into the mascarpone mixture off the heat. Note: the sauce will clump up if it is gets too hot after the Parmesan is added so be careful.
- Adjust the sauce consistency to your likes with heavy cream added in small amounts.
- Season with salt and white pepper to taste.
- Serve sauce over the drained ravioli, and don't be afraid to add more Parmesan on top if you like.

47. Maltese Ravioli Recipe

Serving: 2 | Prep: | Cook: 10mins | Ready in:

Ingredients

- For the Dough:
- 200g plain flour
- a pinch of salt
- 150g semolina
- 2 beaten eggs
- For the filling:
- 400g ricotta
- salt and pepper
- 2 eggs beaten
- 4tbsp grated parmesan cheese
- 1 tbsp chopped parsley

Direction

- Mix the sieved flour, semolina and salt carefully, add the eggs and knead until dough is like elastic, if to stiff add a drop of cold water.
- Rest the dough for 1 hour and prepare the filling.
- Put all the other ingredients ricotta, beaten eggs cheese parsley salt and pepper into a mixing bowl mix everything well.
- Divide the dough into 4 pieces and roll into long thin strips dampen the edges with water.
- Put small balls of ricotta some 2cm from the edge of the pastry and 4cm apart.
- Turn one edge of the pastry on the other one and press to seal, using a ravioli cutter cut out the pastry 10 cm. away from the filling.
- Leave to nest for few minutes, boil in salted water till soft.
- Serve with tomato sauce and grated cheese

48. Manti Turkish Ravioli With Yogurt Sauce Recipe

Serving: 4 | Prep: | Cook: 10mins | Ready in:

Ingredients

- • 1 teaspoon salt
- • 1 teaspoon dried mint
- • 1 (9 ounce) package beef ravioli
- • 1/4 cup butter
- • 1 teaspoon sweet paprika
- • 1 tablespoon minced garlic
- • 1 (8 ounce) container plain whole milk yogurt

Direction

- Bring a large pot of water to a boil. Add salt, mint, and ravioli. Cook for 3 to 5 minutes until the ravioli float to the top, then drain and keep warm.
- Meanwhile, melt butter in a small saucepan over low heat. Stir in paprika, and keep warm as the ravioli are cooking. Stir garlic into the yogurt.
- To serve, place the drained ravioli onto a serving platter or individual plates. Spoon the yogurt on top of the ravioli, then ladle paprika butter over top.

49. Mock Ravioli Recipe

Serving: 12 | Prep: | Cook: 45mins | Ready in:

Ingredients

- 2 medium white onions chopped
- 1 clove garlic minced
- 1 pound ground round
- 1 small can mushroom sauce
- 1 can tomato paste
- 1 can tomato sauce
- 1 cup water
- 1/2 teaspoon salt
- 1 teaspoon freshly ground black pepper
- 1/2 teaspoon italian seasoning
- 1 package chopped frozen spinach cooked
- 1/4 cup minced parsley
- 1/4 cup grated Italian cheese
- 1 teaspoon salt
- 2 eggs beaten
- 1-1/2 teaspoons spaghetti seasoning
- 12 ounces cooked egg noodles

Direction

- With a small amount of oil in a frying pan brown onions, garlic and beef then drain well.
- Stir in mushroom sauce, tomato paste, tomato sauce, water, salt, pepper and seasoning.
- Simmer for 15 minutes.
- Combine spinach, parsley Italian cheese, salt, eggs and spaghetti seasoning.
- Add 1/2 of the meat sauce to the spinach mixture.
- In greased rectangular baking dish arrange one layer of noodles and cover with spinach mixture.
- Alternate combining mixtures until all ingredients are used.
- Cover top with remaining meat sauce and bake at 350 for 45 minutes.
- During the last ten minutes sprinkle with grated cheese and continue baking.

50. Mushroom And Chestnut Raviolis Recipe

Serving: 6 | Prep: | Cook: 4hours3mins | Ready in:

Ingredients

- 1 pasta.html">Homemade pasta
- 1 egg for egg wash
- 500g (1 pound) frozen chestnuts peeled and blanched
- 1 1/2 cups chicken stock
- 4 sprigs of thyme
- 320 gr (11 oz) brown mushrooms
- 130 gr (4.5 oz) unsalted butter
- 2 teaspoons sea salt
- cracked pepper
- 4 tablespoons chopped sage
- 6 tablespoons mascarpone

Direction

- Start by making the pasta.
- Place thawed chestnuts in a small pot with the thyme and chicken stock. Poach on a very low simmer for ten minutes or until tender.
- Chop the mushrooms and melt the butter in the sauté pan. Sauté the mushrooms with 1 teaspoon of sea salt, chopped sage and freshly cracked pepper.
- Strain the chestnuts and combine the mushrooms and chestnuts together. In a food processor reduce the mushrooms and chestnuts to a puree. Adding back two tablespoons of stock to create a smooth paste if needed, fold in mascarpone. Chill until very firm. Season to taste with more sea salt and freshly cracked pepper if necessary.
- Place the pasta sheets on a board with the filling piled high (about 1 and a half tbsp. in the centre of the pasta sheet.
- Egg wash the outside of the base and gently place a second pasta sheet on top pressing the edges down firmly.
- Chill for 2 hours before cooking.

- Poach gently till the ravioli floats to the surface, turn over with slotted spoon to make sure both sides of the won ton wrappers are cooked.
- (All in all about 3 to 5 minutes)
- Serve with a butter sauce, halved cherry tomatoes and fresh mozzarella cheese.

51. Mushroom Ravioli Recipe

Serving: 6 | Prep: | Cook: 10mins | Ready in:

Ingredients

- 8 oz button mushrooms
- 1 tbsp butter
- 1 medium-sized shallot
- 1 small bunch of chives
- 1 ½ tbsp salt
- 4-6 oz skim ricotta cheese
- 48 wonton wrappers
- water
- canola oil for pan frying

Direction

- In a food processor, add button mushrooms (cut in quarters), shallot, and chives and pulse until finely chopped.
- Heat butter in a small saucepan.
- Add mushroom mixture and salt, stirring occasionally until the mushrooms turn a light shade of brown and the shallot is translucent. Make sure it's kind of salty – you'll be adding ricotta to the ravioli, and if the mushroom mixture isn't salty, your ravioli will be bland.
- Spoon 1 tsp. of the mushroom mix on the middle of a wonton, then top with 1 tsp. ricotta cheese.
- Moisten the edge of the wrapper with water, bring two opposite corners together and form a triangle. It's better if you work from the middle of the wonton and push out – this will push out air pockets.
- Repeat until all wontons are used.
- Heat canola oil in a large pan (over med-high heat).
- Add ravioli.
- Flip the ravioli after about 90 seconds.
- Cook for another 30 seconds and add about 2 tbsp. of water to the pan. Turn heat down to medium.
- Cover and cook for another 2-3 minutes.
- Serve with marinara for dipping or with your favorite tomato or white sauce as you would boiled ravioli.

52. Mushroom Ravioli Stuffing Recipe

Serving: 4 | Prep: | Cook: 25mins | Ready in:

Ingredients

- 3 cups finely chopped mixed mushrooms
- 1/2 an onion finely chopped
- 1 package frozen spinach, thawed
- 1/3 cup ricotta cheese
- 2 tbsp garlic infused olive oil
- salt and pepper to taste

Direction

- Put oil in hot pan and begin sautéing the onions until they become transparent. Make sure they do not burn or become too brown.
- Add the mushrooms. Sauté until reduced to almost half.
- Add spinach and heat through.
- Remove from heat and stir in ricotta cheese.
- Season with salt and pepper to taste.

53. Mushroom And Cheese Ravioli With Smoked Tomato Cream Sauce Recipe

Serving: 3 | Prep: | Cook: 30mins | Ready in:

Ingredients

- Fresh pasta (and I'm swiping this from Batali; it also makes far more than you'll need, but fresh pasta is a wonderful thing):
- 3.5 C AP flour
- 4 extra large eggs
- For the filling:
- 8 oz full fat ricotta
- 1/4 C romano or parmesan
- 8 oz mushrooms, minced
- 1-2 shallots, minced
- 2 T butter
- For the sauce:
- ~1C heavy cream
- moderate handful of smoked tomatoes*
- salt and pepper to taste in both the sauce and filling
- *I smoked the tomatoes myself; I made these by mostly dehydrating them then sticking them over low temperature but intense smoke. To be exact I used Mortgage Lifter and Amish Paste (heirloom varieties that aren't too sweet when fresh) tomatoes over a charcoal fire adding fresh wet hickory every 30-45 minutes or so for 2 hours without letting the temperature get past 200 F in the smoker. If the tomatoes weren't sufficiently dry for cabinet storage after the smoker I dehydrated them further until crisp.

Direction

- Pasta:
- Make a well in the pasta, add in the eggs and beat the eggs.
- Mix in the flour, adjusting flour/water so you have a just slightly sticky pasta.
- Knead for 10 minutes, adding flour as necessary.
- Let's be honest, you didn't knead it enough, knead it some more.
- Let it rest for 20 minutes.
- Now, you can either use a pasta maker, or a rolling pin. If using a rolling pin you might as well double the prep time, and you'll have to guess about the thickness of the dough, because I did all this using the settings on my pasta maker.
- Start on the thickest setting, run the dough through, run it through again, fold it in half lengthwise, run it through, then run it through again (flouring as necessary).
- Repeat that for each setting on the pasta maker until you reach either the next to thinnest or thinnest setting (depending on the amount of pasta you want to your filling and how much chew you want). This develops the gluten and makes for a somewhat chewy (when al dente) pasta to contrast with a creamy sauce and filling.
- Filling:
- Melt the butter then sauté the shallot.
- Add in the mushrooms, salt and pepper (keep in mind the Romano will add to the salt), and sauté over medium or medium low until you've cooked pretty much all the moisture out of the mushrooms.
- Allow the mushrooms to cool some, before adding them to the ricotta and Romano and food processing to thoroughly combine.
- Check and adjust seasoning.
- Sauce:
- Toss the cream and the smoked tomatoes in a sauce pan and bring to a low simmer (don't let it come to a full boil). Keep it here for about 20 minutes.
- Add salt and pepper, then puree either with a blender or stick blender. The tomatoes should provide all the thickening agent the sauce needs, but a little Romano could be okay if it's not quite there.
- Assembly:
- Cut the pasta sheet in half, and on one half space out teaspoons worth of the filling leaving enough room to cut individual ravioli.
- Seal the other sheet of pasta on top (which may require a little water or egg wash if your pasta is dry, you want a solid seal), trying to minimize the amount of air around the filling.
- Cut the pasta using an appropriately sized ring mold or similar (or even a sharp knife if that's all you have, but then be prepared to increment up the prep time).

- Cook:
- Dump the ravioli in a large amount of salted water at a high boil, and cook to desired doneness (I tend to go for quite al dente).
- Spoon the sauce on top, sprinkle a little parmesan and maybe some chopped parsley and serve.
- *Additional notes: This is the alpha version of this recipe (came up with it tonight), and all amounts are approximate. That said, the way it turned out, I'd crawl across broken glass for seconds. This also strikes me as a recipe where you could do everything except the sauce and the cooking of the finished ravioli the day before, or even freeze the uncooked ravioli so you could cook the ravioli and make the sauce in a few minutes for a short notice special dish.

- Cook while stirring for 2 minutes or until the zucchini is cooked to desired texture, then add chicken broth.
- Simmer sauce for 2 minutes.
- Season with salt and cracked black pepper to taste.
- PASTA PREPARATION: Prepare pasta when sauce is complete.
- Use a large pot to boil pasta.
- Cook the pasta in salted boiling water until they float (approximately 3 minutes or 160 degrees F internal temperature).
- Remove pasta from boiling water and lightly mix with sauce.
- PLATING SUGGESTION: Place sauced pasta on serving plate then top with grated Parmesan and Parsley.
- Tip: Toss the pasta in a small amount of olive oil after cooking to prevent sticking.

54. Olive Garden Cheese Ravioli With Fresh Vegetables Recipe

Serving: 4 | Prep: | Cook: 25mins | Ready in:

Ingredients

- 1 lb mini round cheese ravioli
- 1/4 cup extra virgin olive oil
- 1 clove fresh garlic, chopped
- 2 (7 ounce) jars roasted red peppers, sliced in strips
- 1 cup fresh zucchini, slice moons
- 1/2 cup black olives, sliced
- 1 cup chicken broth
- grated parmesan cheese
- garnish with chopped fresh parsley
- salt & freshly ground black pepper

Direction

- SAUCE PREPARATION: Heat olive oil over medium heat in saucepan.
- Add roasted red pepper strips, zucchini moons and black olives.

55. Otterpond Sausage Ravioli Recipe

Serving: 12 | Prep: | Cook: 15mins | Ready in:

Ingredients

- 3 cooked sausage Lean turkey italian sausage (sweet)
- 1/4 cup Fresh oregano
- 1/4 cup parsley
- 1 cup Plain bread Crumbs
- 1 1/2 cup cottage cheese Fat Free
- 1/2 cup Freshly Grated parmesan cheese
- 1 egg egg
- 1 egg egg yolk
- 120 wrapper wonton wrapper
- 1 tbsp water
- 1 large egg white egg white

Direction

- In a Cuisinart grind together the cooked sausage and fresh herbs. This will make a crumbly mix.

- Separate the whites from one egg and add the tablespoon of water and set aside for using in an egg wash.
- Put the sausage mixture into a bowl and combine with all remaining ingredients.
- Layout wax paper on the counter so you can separate rows of the wonton wrappers. Using a basting brush, paint the egg wash on each wrapper.
- Brush each wrapper with the egg wash, put a teaspoon of filling in the center of the wrapper and cover with another wrapper.
- Using a ravioli cutter, pound down on it to join the two wrappers, remove the excess wonton and set aside. Repeat this until it's all done.
- These freeze really nicely. I made single server portions and used my FoodSaver to package them up for the freezer.
- To cook, gently float the ravioli in furiously boiling water and let cook for about 5-10 minutes or until they float up. Serve with a simple tomato sauce and green salad.

56. Pelmeni Russian Ravioli Recipe

Serving: 2 | Prep: | Cook: 20mins | Ready in:

Ingredients

- **FILLING**
- ¼ lb beef mince (i used kangaroo mince because its cheaper and healthier...hardly russian but whatever)
- ¼ lb pork mince
- 1 brown onion, finely chopped
- 1 tsp nutmeg
- salt
- pepper
- ***DOUGH***
- 1 ¼ cups flour
- 3 eggs
- warm water, as needed
- ***SAUCE***
- ½ brown onion, chopped
- 2 cloves garlic, crushed
- 2 Tbsp red wine vinegar
- 400g tin tomatoes
- 2 tbsp chopped dill pickles
- 1 tsp dill
- ****
- sour cream and extra pickles to serve

Direction

- - Make the filling: Combine everything in a food processor. Place in fridge until needed.
- - Make the dough: Place flour in a mound on a clean surface, create a well in the middle, crack eggs into the well and use your hands to combine. Add water as needed to form a soft, but not sticky, dough. Knead until smooth. Wrap in plastic and let rest in the fridge 30 minutes.
- - Make the sauce: Sauté onion and garlic in a small saucepan with a little oil until soft. Add vinegar and bring to a boil. Add remaining ingredients, boil and simmer until it's thickish. (8 – 10 minutes).
- - Make the pelmeni: Roll the dough into a long snake shape about an inch thick. Cut off about an inch of the snake and roll flat into a circle. Place a small amount of filling in the circle and fold to enclose. Seal well.
- - Cook the pelmeni: Boil a big pot of salted water. Add the pelmeni. Cook, stirring a bit so they don't stick to the bottom. When they float to the top and stay there, they are cooked.
- - Serve the pelmeni: Drain and serve on a plate or bowl, top with warm sauce and sour cream and extra pickles.

57. Pesto Ravioli With Goat Cheese And Walnuts Recipe

Serving: 4 | Prep: | Cook: 30mins | Ready in:

Ingredients

- 18 ounce bag frozen pesto flavored ravioli
- 2 tablespoons unsalted butter
- 4 ounce log goat cheese crumbled
- 2 tablespoons julienned fresh basil leaves
- 2 tablespoons chopped walnuts or pine nuts toasted

Direction

- Prepare ravioli according to package instructions.
- Reserve 1/2 cup of pasta cooking water before draining.
- Meanwhile in large skillet over low heat melt butter.
- When butter is just melted add goat cheese and stir to combine.
- Add 1/3 cup reserved cooking liquid stirring until creamy and thick.
- Add cooked ravioli to skillet and stir to coat with sauce adding more water if necessary.
- Season with salt and pepper then add basil and stir to combine.
- Transfer to serving bowl and sprinkle with walnuts.

58. Philly Cheesesteak Ravioli Recipe

Serving: 6 | Prep: | Cook: 30mins | Ready in:

Ingredients

- For Filling
- 1/2lb minced beef rib eye
- 1 bell pepper, finely diced
- 1 onion, finely diced
- a clove garlic, minced
- a few fresh mushrooms, finely diced
- drizzle of olive oil
- kosher or sea salt and fresh ground pepper
- For Cheese Sauce
- 1/2 stick butter
- 3 cups milk(plus a lil more if sauce is too thick after adding the cheese)
- 1/2 cup flour
- 1 1/2t dry mustard
- 4oz cream cheese, softened, or even warmed in microwave(you want NO chill on this at all)
- 4-5 cups sharp cheddar cheese, shredded(don't use the preshredded, make sure to shred your own!)
- homemade ravioli dough or Asian dumpling wrappers

Direction

- For Filling
- Heat olive oil in a medium skillet over medium heat
- Add onion pepper and cook about 5 minutes
- Add garlic, mushrooms, salt and pepper and beef and cook another 5 or so.
- Set aside, keeping warm
- For Cheese Sauce
- Melt butter in medium, heavy pan over medium low heat.
- Add dry mustard and flour and stir to make a simple roux.
- Add cream milk and cream cheese and stir until beginning to thicken.
- Cook a few minutes then add shredded cheese, stirring constantly until melted and sauce is thick and smooth. Set aside and keep on warm.
- For Ravioli
- Set a large pot of water to boil
- Using a small slotted spoon or fork, add about 1t or so of beef/veggie filling to pasta pieces, wet edges and top with another piece, pressing edges together well.
- Drop 4-6 ravioli into boiling water at a time.
- Ravioli should be done when it floats to the surface. These should only take a few minutes
- Serve with warmed cheese sauce.
- I topped mine with fried jalapeno strips for a little crunch.

59. Portobello Mushroom Ravioli With Prawns Recipe

Serving: 6 | Prep: | Cook: 15mins | Ready in:

Ingredients

- 20 large prawns, peeled and deveined
- 12 ounces prepared fresh cheese ravioli
- 7 large portobello mushrooms, sliced
- 3 cloves garlic, minced
- 3 tablespoons capers
- 3/8 cup butter
- 5 fluid ounces white wine
- 2 tablespoons olive oil
- freshly ground black pepper
- 2 tablespoons grated parmesan cheese
- 1/2 lemon, juiced

Direction

- Have a stock pot of water near boiling before starting the sauce for this recipe! If you're fast at making the sauce, throw in ravioli when you begin to make the sauce. If not, cook ravioli according to package directions.
- In a large saucepan, melt 1/4 cup of butter or margarine over a medium heat. Sauté garlic for 1 to 2 minutes. Stir in olive oil and capers. Add 4 ounces of white wine and prawns, and bring to a boil.
- Reduce heat and simmer for 2 to 3 minutes, letting wine reduce. Stir in sliced mushrooms, and additional butter and wine so that the sauce is thick, but still liquid after 2 to 3 minutes. Stir in lemon juice, and add fresh pepper to taste.
- To serve, place raviolis on 4 plates, then place 5 to 6 prawns on each plate. Evenly distribute the remaining sauce between the four plates, and garnish with lots of freshly grated parmesan cheese!

60. Potato Ravioli With Braised Leeks And Potato Crisp Recipe

Serving: 4 | Prep: | Cook: 2hours | Ready in:

Ingredients

- 2 large potatoes, peeled
- 1 egg, lightly beaten
- micro basil and finely grated Parmesan, to serve
- Mashed potato:
- 1/4 cup coarse rock salt
- 2 Sebago potatoes
- 2 tbs olive oil
- Chlorophyll:
- 100g baby spinach, washed and drained
- 75g flat leaf parsley leaves
- pasta dough:
- 100g '00' flour, plus extra for dusting
- 1 whole egg
- 1 tsp extra virgin olive oil
- 25g chlorophyll
- Braised leeks
- 20g butter
- 2 leeks, white part only, halved, core removed, diced into 1cm pieces
- 2 sprigs thyme
- 100ml chicken stock
- potato crisp :
- 2 large Sebago potatoes, peeled and washed
- 1/3cup corn flour
- 1/4 cup clarified butter

Direction

- Preheat an oven to 180C.
- For the mashed potato, scatter the rock salt over the base of a baking tray then prick potatoes with a fork. Place on top of the salt and bake for 1-1 1/2 hours until tender. While the potatoes are hot, peel and push them through a potato ricer, then stir through the olive oil and season with sea salt. Set aside until needed.
- For the chlorophyll, add the spinach and parsley to a blender with 400ml of water and a

generous pinch of salt. Blend the mixture to a puree, then pour into a saucepan. Gently bring the mixture to a boil, then skim the green chlorophyll from the surface and strain through a damp muslin cloth in a sieve, set over a bowl filled with ice, to cool quickly. Squeeze out excess liquid and reserve.
- To make the pasta dough, place flour, eggs, olive oil, chlorophyll and a pinch of salt into a food processor. Pulse until the dough starts to come together. Tip the dough onto a clean work surface, lightly dusted in flour and knead for a few minutes until the dough is firm and elastic. Wrap in cling wrap and leave to rest in the fridge for 1 hour.
- Remove dough from the fridge and divide in half. Form each piece into a rectangular shape. Dust the pasta rollers with flour and turn to the largest setting. Feed pasta through the rollers, folding the dough into 3 after changing each setting. Roll dough out to the 2nd thinnest setting. Repeat with remaining dough and cover with a damp tea towel.
- Use a mandolin or sharp knife to slice potato thinly. Cut into 4 x 6cm pieces. Blanch the potato pieces in salted, simmering water for about 1-2 minutes until just tender. Refresh in iced water and set aside.
- For the braised leeks, melt the butter in a small saucepan over medium heat. Add the leeks and thyme and cook for 3-4 minutes until softened. Season with salt. Add chicken stock, reduce heat to medium-low and cover with a lid. Cook for a further 6-8 minutes or until leeks are very tender.
- To make the potato crisp, use a potato turner and slicer to turn the potato into potato 'spaghetti'. Transfer to a large bowl. Coat the potato in the corn flour and season well with sea salt. Arrange potato 'spaghetti' in a small frying pan. Spoon over the clarified butter and gently cook over medium heat for about 5 minutes each side until golden. Season with salt and place on a wire rack to cool and dry out.
- To make the ravioli, transfer the mash potato to a piping bag. Pipe a mound of potato onto each potato slice. Lay a piece of pasta onto a clean work surface and brush with egg. Cut pasta into individual squares allowing 1.5 cm extra around the rectangular piece of potato. Pipe some of the potato filling onto the centre of each potato slice. Cut the remaining pasta sheet to size. Carefully shape pasta to fit mashed potato mound, making a fold at one side. Brush with a little extra egg to seal. Place on a lightly floured tray and put in the fridge for 5-10 minutes to rest.
- Cook the ravioli in a large saucepan of salted boiling water for 3-5 minutes until al dente.
- To serve, divide braised leeks and ravioli between serving bowls. Scatter over micro basil, top with potato crisps and sprinkle over Parmesan.

61. Pumpkin Ravioli Recipe

Serving: 6 | Prep: | Cook: 15mins | Ready in:

Ingredients

- 1 cup ricotta cheese
- 1/2 cup pumpkin puree
- 1/2 teaspoon salt
- 1/4 teaspoon ground nutmeg
- 2 cups all-purpose flour
- 1/2 teaspoon salt
- 1/4 cup tomato paste
- 1 tablespoon olive oil
- 2 eggs
- 2 tablespoons water

Direction

- Mix the cheese, pumpkin, 1/2 teaspoon salt, and the nutmeg. Set filling aside.
- Mix the flour, and 1/2 teaspoon salt in a large bowl; make a well in the center of the flour. Beat the tomato paste, oil, and eggs until well blended, and pour into the well in the flour. Stir with a fork, gradually bring the flour mixture to the center of the bow until the

dough makes a ball. If the dough is too dry, mix in up to 2 tablespoons water.
- Knead lightly on a floured cloth-covered surface, adding flour if dough is sticky, until smooth and elastic, about 5 minutes. Cover, and let rest for another 5 minutes. Divide the dough into 4 equal parts. Roll the dough, one part at a time, into a rectangle about 12 x 10 inches. Keep the rest of the dough covered while working.
- Drop 2 level teaspoons filling onto half of the rectangle, about 1 1/2 inches apart in 2 rows of 4 mounds each. Moisten the edges of the dough, and the dough between the rows of pumpkin mixture with water. Fold the other half of the dough up over the pumpkin mixture, pressing the dough down around the pumpkin. Cut between the rows of filling to make ravioli; press the edges together with a fork, or cut with a pastry wheel. Seal edges well. Repeat with the remaining dough and pumpkin filling. Place ravioli on towel. Let stand, turning once, until dry, about 30 minutes.
- Cook ravioli in 4 quarts of boiling salted water until tender; drain carefully.
- Serve with Pumpkin Seed Pesto!

62. Pumpkin Ravioli W Hazelnut Cream Recipe

Serving: 6 | Prep: | Cook: 45mins |Ready in:

Ingredients

- 2 1/2 cups pumpkin puree
- 2 large carrots, cooked and pureed
- 2 onions, diced
- 1 clove garlic, minced
- 2 teaspoons ground coriander seed
- 1/2 teaspoon ground mace
- 1/2 teaspoon ground allspice
- 1 pinch ground cardamom
- 1 cup unsalted butter
- 1/3 pound grated parmesan cheese
- 2 tablespoons real maple syrup
- 1 egg, beaten
- 2 1/2 pounds fresh pasta sheets
- salt to taste
- ground black pepper to taste
- 1 cup hazelnuts
- 3 cups heavy whipping cream
- 3 cloves garlic, minced
- 1 pinch cayenne pepper
- 1 pinch white pepper
- salt to taste
- 2 cups shredded sorrel, stems removed

Direction

- Preheat the oven to 400 degrees F (205 degrees C). Toast the hazelnuts in a shallow pan on the middle rack for 10 to 12 minutes, or until brown and fragrant. When they are cool enough to handle, wrap the nuts tightly in a lint-free towel, and vigorously rub nuts against the towel. Continue rubbing until the nuts are almost blond.
- Sauté the onions, garlic, and spices in butter or margarine until the onions are soft. Stir together with the pureed vegetables. Add cheese, maple syrup, egg, salt, and black pepper. Adjust seasoning. Set the filling aside.
- Cook the cream, garlic, cayenne, and white pepper over high heat; stir often, and adjust heat to keep the cream from boiling over. When the cream is thick enough to coat the back of a spoon, add a pinch salt. Adjust seasoning. Remove sauce from heat until you're ready to use it.
- Lay one sheet of Fresh Pasta out on a flat surface. Spray with water to prevent drying, and to make it more flexible. Place half tablespoons of filling along the bottom edge of the pasta about 1/2 inch apart. For larger ravioli, use 1 tablespoon of filling, and leave 1 inch between dollops. Fold the pasta sheet over the filling, and cut apart with a ravioli cutter. Set the finished ravioli aside, and cover with a damp cloth. Repeat until filling and/or pasta is completely used.

- Cook the ravioli in salted boiling water until al dente. Drain.
- Meanwhile, reheat the sauce. Add the shredded sorrel to the sauce; cook just until it wilts -- about 30 seconds. Add half the hazelnuts, turn the heat off, and add the cooked ravioli. Stir gently, and serve immediately. Garnish with remaining hazelnuts.

63. Pumpkin Raviolis Recipe

Serving: 8 | Prep: | Cook: 5mins | Ready in:

Ingredients

- For Raviolis:
- 1 can (15 1/2 ounces) white beans (great Northern, navy or cannellini beans), drained and rinsed
- 1/4 cup toasted pine nuts
- 2 cloves garlic
- 1 can (15 ounces) 100% pure pumpkin
- 1 teaspoon kosher salt
- 1/4 teaspoon ground, black pepper
- 3/4 cup grated parmesan cheese
- 1 extra-large egg
- 48 refrigerated or frozen Chinese dumpling skins (about 1 pound)
- water for sealing raviolis
- 1 teaspoon white vinegar
- 20 drops yellow food color or dye
- 10 drops red food color or dye
- For Sauce:
- 6 tablespoons salted butter or margarine
- 1 garlic clove, minced
- 6 tablespoons shredded parmesan cheese
- 24 parsley sprigs, preferable flat-leaf parsley

Direction

- Purée beans, pine nuts and garlic in food processor until smooth. Combine with pumpkin, salt, pepper, Parmesan cheese and egg.
- To make ravioli, place 1 1/2 tablespoons filling in the center of a dumpling skin, moisten edges with water and top with another dumpling skin. Press edges firmly to seal, being careful to push all air out of ravioli before sealing pasta completely around filling. Crimp edges with a fork; repeat until all raviolis are formed.
- Mix vinegar and food color. Paint raviolis the color of pumpkins with a small paintbrush. Let dry for at least 5 minutes; add a second coat and dry for 10 minutes more.
- Heat a large pot of lightly salted water to boiling. Boil raviolis for about 3 minutes and drain.
- While raviolis are cooking, melt butter in small skillet with garlic. Toss with drained raviolis and sprinkle with Parmesan cheese. Arrange on plates and place parsley around pumpkins like stems.
- Nutritional Information Per Serving: Calories 410; Total fat 17g; Saturated fat 8g; Cholesterol 70mg; Sodium 820mg; Carbohydrate 51g; Fiber 6g; Protein 16g. Vitamin A 170%DV*; Vitamin C 8%DV; Calcium 20%DV; Iron 25%DV
- * Daily Value
- COURTESY OF MEALTIME.ORG

64. Pumpkin Seed Pesto With Pumpkin Ravioli Recipe

Serving: 8 | Prep: | Cook: 15mins | Ready in:

Ingredients

- 1/2 cup hulled pumpkin seeds (green best)
- 1 1/2 cup packed parsley (fresh)
- 1 small clove garlic
- 1/2 cup EVOO
- 1/2 cup parmesan (fresh, grated)
- 1/4 tsp cayenne pepper
- 1/4 tsp ground cinnamon
- salt

- 2 lbs pumkin ravioli (see other recipe)

Direction

- Bring pot of salted water to a boil. Preheat oven to 350 degrees F. Spread pumpkin seeds on rimmed backing sheet and toast for 5 minutes. Let cool.
- Combine seeds, parsley, and garlic in food processor and process until finely chopped. With motor running, add oil in a steady stream and process until smooth, scraping down sides of bowl as necessary. Scrap mixture into a bowl and stir Parmesan, cayenne, and cinnamon. Season with salt. Pesto will be thick.
- Cook ravioli according to directions. Set aside one cup of pasta cooking water, drain ravioli, and return to pot. Gently stir in pesto and enough reserved water to moisten ravioli. Serve immediately.

65. Quick Ravioli Bake Recipe

Serving: 4 | Prep: | Cook: 35mins | Ready in:

Ingredients

- 1 lb lean ground beef
- 1 onion - chopped
- 2 cloves garlic - minced
- 1/2 tsp salt
- 1/4 tsp pepper
- 1 can (28oz / 796ml) diced tomatoes
- 1 tsp dried Italian herb seasoning or oregano
- 1 lb fresh or frozen ravioli or tortellini
- 1/2 cup shredded mozzarella cheese
- 1/4 cup grated parmesan cheese

Direction

- In a large non-stick skillet, cook beef over med-high heat, breaking up with wooden spoon, until no longer pink. 5 - 7 mins. Drain off fat.
- Add onion, garlic, salt & pepper & cook for 5 mins.
- Stir in tomatoes & herb seasoning.
- Reduce heat to med-low, cover & cook for 10 mins.
- Meanwhile in a large saucepan of boiling salted water, cook ravioli for 2 - 5 mins if fresh, 6 - 8 mins if frozen, or until tender but still firm.
- Drain well & add to sauce, tossing well to coat.
- Divide among 4 individual gratin dishes or place in 1 - 11 x 7 in glass baking dish.
- Sprinkle with cheeses.
- Bake in a 450 degree oven until cheeses have melted, about 10 mins

66. Ravioli Alfredo With Shrimp Recipe

Serving: 6 | Prep: | Cook: 30mins | Ready in:

Ingredients

- 1 pkg (24 oz) frozen, large,round cheese ravioli
- 4 plum tomatoes,chopped, (2 cups)
- 2 cloves garlic,crushed
- 2 Tbs olive oil
- 1/4 c sliced fresh basil
- 2 Tbs white balsamic vinegar
- 1/8 tsp pepper
- 1 small red onion,diced (1/4c)
- 18 medium shrimp (3/4 lb),peeled and deveined,tails left on
- 1 jar (16 oz) alfredo sauce

Direction

- Cook ravioli according to pkg. directions.
- Meanwhile, in bowl, toss tomatoes with half of garlic, 1 Tbsp. oil, sliced basil, vinegar and pepper; reserve.
- In large non-stick skillet, heat remaining 1 Tbsp. oil over medium heat
- Add remaining garlic, onion and shrimp; cook, stirring until shrimp are lightly browned, 4 to

5 mins. Stir in Alfredo sauce and 1/4 cup water. Bring to simmer, cook 4 mins, stirring occasionally. Drain the ravioli, add to skillet. Cook, stirring gently for 3 mins

- Serve shrimp and ravioli with reserved tomato-basil mixture. Garnish with additional basil.
- Note: The second time I made this, I found I liked the tomato mixture added in the dish the last minute or two so it warms up, instead of serving cold on top.

67. Ravioli Casserole Recipe

Serving: 8 | Prep: | Cook: 40mins | Ready in:

Ingredients

- 28-oz. jar spaghetti sauce, divided (or your own homemade sauce)
- 25-oz. pkg. frozen cheese ravioli, cooked and divided
- 16-oz. container ricotta cheese, divided
- 16-oz. pkg. shredded mozzarella cheese, divided
- 1/4 c. fresh grated parmesan cheese

Direction

- Spread 1/2 cup spaghetti sauce in a lightly greased 13" x 9" baking pan; layer with half the ravioli. Pour 1-1/4 cups sauce over ravioli. Spread one cup cottage cheese over top; sprinkle with 2 cups mozzarella cheese. Layer with remaining ingredients, ending with mozzarella cheese. Sprinkle with Parmesan cheese. Bake, uncovered, at 350 degrees for 30 to 40 minutes. Let stand for 5 to 10 minutes before serving..

68. Ravioli Casserole In The Crockpot Recipe

Serving: 4 | Prep: | Cook: 480mins | Ready in:

Ingredients

- 1-1/2 pounds lean ground beef
- 1 medium white onion chopped
- 2 garlic cloves minced
- 28 ounce can peeled tomatoes in thick puree
- 15 ounce can tomato sauce
- 2 teaspoons Italian herb seasoning
- 1/4 teaspoon freshly ground black pepper
- 1 pound bow tie pasta freshly cooked
- 10 ounces frozen chopped spinach thawed and squeezed dry
- 2 cups ricotta cheese
- 1/2 cup freshly grated imported parmesan cheese

Direction

- In a large skillet over medium high heat cook the ground beef, onion and garlic stirring often to break up lumps for 5 minutes. Tilt pan to drain off excess fat then transfer beef mixture to a small slow cooker. Add tomatoes with their puree, tomato sauce, Italian seasoning and pepper stirring to break up tomatoes with the side of a spoon. Cover and slow cook for 8 hours on low. Skim the fat from the surface of the meat sauce then stir in the cooked pasta, spinach, ricotta and Parmesan cheese and slow cook for 5 minutes.

69. Ravioli Lasagna Recipe

Serving: 8 | Prep: | Cook: 60mins | Ready in:

Ingredients

- 2 bags 9about 20 oz ea) square ravioli(I use spinach and cheese)
- 4-3/4 c spaghetti sauce,divided

- 3 TB grated Parmesan cheese
- 3 c (12 oz) Mozzarella cheese

Direction

- Preheat oven to 350"
- In large pot of boiling salted water, cook ravioli to desired doneness; drain (I have skipped this and just thawed the raviolis also).
- Pour 1 c spaghetti sauce in bottom of 9x13" baking dish. Layer 1/3 of raviolis on top of sauce, sprinkle with 1 TB Parmesan cheese, pour 1-1/4 c of sauce over it, and then cover with 1 c mozzarella cheese.
- Repeat the layers two more times.
- Bake 35-40 mins covered. Uncover and cook 10-15 mins. more until golden. Cool 15 mins before serving.

70. Ravioli Lasange Recipe

Serving: 6 | Prep: | Cook: 45mins |Ready in:

Ingredients

- 2 bags Frozen Ravioli, or tortellini
- 1 - 2 jars marinara sauce
- 3 - 4 cups Shredded mozzarella cheese
- Shredding Parmesean

Direction

- Grease a 9x13" pan. Layer the uncooked ravioli, sauce, and cheese.
- Repeat until all ingredients are gone (3 to 4 layers).
- Bake at 350°F until cheese is melted (30 to 45 minutes).

71. Ravioli Marinara Recipe

Serving: 6 | Prep: | Cook: 20mins |Ready in:

Ingredients

- 1 package (25 to 27 1/2 oz) frozen cheese-filled ravioli
- 1 jar (28 oz) tomato pasta sauce (any chunky variety)
- 1 bag (1 lb) frozen broccoli, green beans, pearl onions and red peppers
- 1 can (15 oz) Progresso® cannellini (white kidney) beans, drained, rinsed
- 1/4 cup shredded fresh parmesan cheese, if desired

Direction

- 1. Cook and drain ravioli as directed on package.
- 2. While ravioli is cooking, mix pasta sauce, vegetables and beans in 3-quart saucepan. Heat to boiling; reduce heat. Simmer uncovered 6 to 8 minutes or until vegetables are tender.
- 3. Serve vegetable mixture over ravioli. Serve with cheese.

72. Ravioli Skillet Lasagna Florentine Recipe

Serving: 4 | Prep: | Cook: 30mins |Ready in:

Ingredients

- 2 cups light chunk-style spaghetti sauce
- 1/3 cup water
- 1 (9 ounce) package cheese ravioli or meat-filled ravioli
- 1 slightly beaten egg
- 1 (15 ounce) carton fat-free ricotta cheese
- 1/4 cup grated romano cheese or parmesan cheese
- 1 (10 ounce) package frozen chopped spinach, thawed and drained
- grated romano cheese or parmesan cheese

Direction

- Mix together egg and ricotta. Pour spaghetti sauce and water into a deep pan and place over moderate heat.
- Boil the ravioli, drain and add to sauce. Fold in ricotta and egg mixture.
- Add thawed spinach and Romano and heat.
- Serve hot.
- Note: If using Alfredo sauce, omit water and use milk in its place.

73. Ravioli Skillet Recipe

Serving: 4 | Prep: | Cook: 9mins | Ready in:

Ingredients

- 1 pound ground beef
- 3/4 cup chopped green pepper
- 1 ounce prosciutto or deli ham, chopped
- 3 cups spaghetti sauce
- 3/4 cup water
- 1 package (25 ounces) frozen cheese ravioli
- 1 cup (4 ounces) shredded part-skim mozzarella cheese

Direction

- In a large skillet, cook the beef, green pepper and prosciutto over medium heat until meat is no longer pink; drain.
- Stir in spaghetti sauce and water; bring to a boil. Add ravioli. Reduce heat; cover and simmer for 7-9 minutes or until ravioli is tender, stirring once. Sprinkle with cheese. Simmer, uncovered, 1-2 minutes longer or until cheese is melted.
- Yield: 4 servings.

74. Ravioli With Balsamic Butter Recipe

Serving: 2 | Prep: | Cook: 30mins | Ready in:

Ingredients

- 18 to 20 oz store bought (frozen works great here) ravioli - ie mushroom spinach is nice.
- 6 Tbsp unsalted butter
- 1/2 tsp salt
- 1/4 tsp fresh ground black pepper
- 1/3 cup toasted, chopped walnuts
- 1/4 cup grated parmesan
- 2 Tbsp balsamic vinegar. (make it a good one)

Direction

- Place the walnuts on a small baking pan, and toast in the oven on broil for a few minutes... not much. Judgement call on this one. Then set aside.
- Bring large pot of salted water to a rapid boil over high heat. Add the ravioli and cook 4 - 5 minutes, until tender but firm to the bite.
- Drain ravioli and place in large platter.
- While the ravioli is cooking, melt and cook the butter in a medium saucepan over medium heat stirring occasionally. When the butter's foam subsides and begins to turn a golden brown (~ 3 minutes) turn off the heat. Let the butter cool ~ 1 minute, then stir in the balsamic vinegar, salt, and pepper.
- Transfer the ravioli to the saucepan with the balsamic brown butter and coat the ravioli thoroughly.
- Sprinkle the toasted walnuts and Parmesan over the Ravioli.
- Serve immediately.

75. Ravioli With Brown Butter And Sage Recipe

Serving: 4 | Prep: | Cook: 20mins | Ready in:

Ingredients

- 1 24-ounce package fresh cheese ravioli
- 6 tablespoons unsalted butter
- 2 medium shallots, thinly sliced

- 16 fresh sage leaves
- 1/4 teaspoon kosher salt
- 1/4 teaspoon black pepper
- 3/4 cup (3 ounces) grated Parmesan

Direction

- Cook the ravioli according to the package directions.
- Meanwhile, heat the butter in a large skillet over medium-low heat until it foams.
- Add the shallots and cook, stirring, until golden, 1 to 2 minutes.
- Increase heat to medium, add the sage, and cook until the leaves turn crisp, about 1 1/2 minutes.
- Remove from heat. Season with the salt and pepper.
- Return the drained ravioli to the pot, add the butter and sage, and toss gently. Add 1/2 cup of the Parmesan and toss again.
- Divide among individual bowls and top with the remaining Parmesan.

76. Ravioli With Creamy Pesto Sauce Recipe

Serving: 5 | Prep: | Cook: 30mins | Ready in:

Ingredients

- 1 cup whipping cream
- 1 (2.82-ounce) jar pesto sauce
- 2 (9-ounce) packages refrigerated cheese-filled ravioli, uncooked
- 2 tablespoons pine nuts, toasted

Direction

- Combine cream and pesto in a medium saucepan.
- Cook over low heat until thoroughly heated, stirring frequently (do not boil).
- Cook pasta according to package directions in salted water; drain. Toss pasta with whipping cream mixture and sprinkle with pine nuts.
- Serve immediately.

77. Ravioli With Gorgonzola Artichoke Hearts And Peas Sauce Recipe

Serving: 2 | Prep: | Cook: 45mins | Ready in:

Ingredients

- 4 artichokes, steamed
- 2 tbs. extra virgin olive oil
- 2-3 cloves garlic, sliced thinly
- 1 tbs. chopped fresh rosemary
- 1/4-1/3 lb. gorgonzola or Cambozola cheese, cut into pieces
- 1/2 cup milk
- 1 cup fresh or frozen English peas
- salt and freshly ground pepper
- Freshly grated Reggiano or other good parmesan cheese
- 1 lb good fresh or frozen ricotta cheese ravioli on which to lavish this sauce...

Direction

- Steam the artichokes, until the leaves pull away easily.
- Discard or gnaw on the leaves of the steamed artichokes, leaving the hearts for the recipe.
- Clean the choke away thoroughly and slice the hearts into small 1/2" pieces.
- Heat the olive oil in a sauté pan over medium heat.
- Sauté the garlic, being careful not to burn it or cook it too brown or crisp.
- Add the chopped rosemary and sauté another minute.
- Reduce the heat to medium low.
- Add the cheese and milk and stir until melted and smooth.

- Reduce the heat further.
- Add the peas and artichoke hearts and cook until bright green.
- Add a little more milk if the sauce has gotten too thick.
- Add salt and freshly ground pepper to taste.
- Pour the sauce over the ravioli, sprinkle grated parmesan on top and serve.
- Any extra sauce may be refrigerated and heated up with a little milk.

78. Ravioli With Spinach Alfredo Recipe

Serving: 1 | Prep: | Cook: 20mins | Ready in:

Ingredients

- 8 large fresh frozen ricotta cheese stuffed raviolis
- 4 cups water
- 2 tbsp olive oil
- 3 tbsp butter
- 1 cup frozen spinach
- 1 tbs basil
- 2 crushed and chopped garlic cloves
- 1 cup milk
- 1 tbsp flour
- 1/2 cup grated parmesean cheese

Direction

- Get into your freezer and pull out the big bad of frozen raviolis that you get at Costco and take out about 7 or 8 of them. Set aside.
- Bring the 4 cups of water to a boil.
- Over low heat put olive oil, butter, and garlic in the skillet and sauté for about 5 minutes.
- Add frozen spinach and basil to the skillet
- In a bowl mix the milk and flour together till there are no lumps
- As soon as the spinach is all thawed out in the skillet and sautéing nicely, add the milk and flour mixture and the parmesan cheese.
- Keep the skillet on low.

- Put the ravioli into the pot with the boiling water.
- When the ravioli floats to the top, they are done
- Drain the ravioli.
- Sauce will begin to thicken very quickly, when it has thickened to desired consistency and cheese is melted, turn heat off.
- Put the ravioli on a plate, pour on the spinach sauce.
- MMMMMMMMMMMMMM!!!!!

79. Ravioli With Spinach Chicken And Ricotta Recipe

Serving: 4 | Prep: | Cook: 10mins | Ready in:

Ingredients

- Fresh pasta sheets, either homemade or bought, for ravioli dough.
- 1 package frozen spinach, thawed and wrung out dry
- 1/2 tsp. fresh lemon zest
- 1/2 lb. ricotta cheese
- 1 egg
- 1 clove garlic, minced.
- 1/2 cup or more romano cheese
- salt, pepper, to taste.
- 1 cup ground up chicken (save from leftovers, or use one of the store bought rotisseries...very simple this way)
- dash of cayenne pepper sauce

Direction

- Have your pasta sheets ready and off to the side. Make sure you have a lightly floured surface to lay the ravioli out in single layers after you press them.
- In a bowl, beat ricotta cheese, egg and Romano till fluffy.
- Mix in spinach, lemon zest, salt and pepper.
- Fold in the chicken and add a dash of the cayenne pepper sauce.

- Place a spoonful (I use a 1 inch ice cream scoop) of filling on dough. Cover with another piece of dough and press with a ravioli cutter, cup, whatever you choose to shape your raviolis. Make sure edges are sealed.
- **Note. I find that laying out a long strip of dough and placing drops of filling across and then covering with another piece of dough and then cutting the ravioli makes for quick work in the kitchen.
- Lay ravioli out in single layers to dry a bit while you clean up and bring your water to a slow boil. At this point you may also freeze for later use. When you are ready, cook for about 6 min. Check at this time and continue to boil if dough is still tough.
- Top with your favorite sauce, or like me, some EVOO and fresh Romano.
- Basic Pasta dough recipes can be found anywhere, and it's really worth giving it a try if you haven't yet. Pasta machines are also inexpensive, you can pick one up for $30, and may find you have a new love for making homemade pasta. Scraps from my ravioli are run thru the spaghetti setting for my kids to eat later.

80. Ravioli With Zucchini And Walnuts Recipe

Serving: 4 | Prep: | Cook: 15mins | Ready in:

Ingredients

- 1 - 9 oz. pkg. refrigerated whole wheat or plain cheese ravioli
- 1/2 c. walnuts, coarsely chopped
- 2 TBSP. extra-virgin olive oil
- 2 medium zucchini, halved lengthwise and sliced
- 6 scallions (green onions), sliced on the diagonal 1/4 inch thick
- 1/2 c. milk
- 1 c. finely shredded parmigiano Reggiano cheese (4 oz.) or grated parmesan cheese, divided
- 1/8 tsp. sea salt
- 1/8 tsp. fresh cracked black pepper

Direction

- In large saucepan, cook refrigerated ravioli according to package directions; drain.
- Meanwhile, in large skillet cook nuts in hot oil over medium heat for 2 to 3 minutes; remove with slotted spoon. Add zucchini and green onion. Cook and stir for 2 to 3 minutes or until crisp-tender.
- Add drained pasta, nuts, milk, and 3/4 c. of cheese to skillet. Cook and toss for 1 minute. Season to taste with salt and pepper. Transfer pasta mixture to serving bowl. Sprinkle with remaining cheese. Serve immediately.

81. Ravioli And Sausage Lasagna Recipe

Serving: 6 | Prep: | Cook: 65mins | Ready in:

Ingredients

- 4 links turkey italian sausage
- 1 (7 oz) jar roasted red peppers
- 1 teaspoon dried basil
- 1 (26 oz) jar marinara sauce
- 1 (30 oz) package large square frozen cheese ravioli, thawed
- 1 cup shredded mozzarella cheese
- 2 tablespoons grated parmesan cheese

Direction

- Heat oven to 375 degrees. You'll need a shallow 2-quart baking dish.
- Heat a medium non-stick skillet over medium-high heat. Add sausages and cook, breaking up chunks with a spoon, 5 minutes or until no

longer pink. Remove from heat; stir in roasted red peppers and basil.
- Spread 1 cup pasta sauce in baking dish. Top with a layer of 12 ravioli, the sausage mixture, and then the mozzarella cheese. Top with 1 cup sauce, remaining ravioli and remaining sauce. Cover with non-stick foil.
- Bake on a sheet of foil (to catch any drips) 1 hour or until ravioli are tender when pierced. Uncover, sprinkle with parmesan cheese and bake 5 minutes until cheese is barely golden. Let stand 15 minutes before serving.

82. Ravioli Con Ricotta E Spinaci Ravioli Stuffed With Spinach And Ricotta Cheese Recipe

Serving: 6 | Prep: | Cook: 20mins | Ready in:

Ingredients

- for the filling
- 1 lb fresh spinach
- 1 lb ricotta cheese, thoroughly drained
- 1 egg
- 4 oz parmigiano reggiano cheese, freshly grated
- salt and pepper
- pinch of nutmeg
- for the dough
- 3 cups flour
- 4 eggs
- 1 tablespoon extra-virgin olive oil
- for the dressing
- 4 oz unsalted butter
- 10 fresh sage leaves
- 4 oz freshly grated parmigiano cheese

Direction

- 1) Boil the spinach in lightly salted water. Place the boiled spinach in a cheese cloth and form a small sack. Squeeze the sack to expel as much water as possible. Chop the spinach finely
- 2) Place the spinach in a bowl. Combine the drained ricotta, egg, Parmigiano cheese, salt, pepper, and a generous pinch of nutmeg. Taste and adjust the salt, pepper, and nutmeg if necessary
- 3) Prepare the pasta dough using the recipe for fresh pasta. Make the dough very soft and moist. Use the minimum flour necessary, just enough to prevent the dough from sticking to your hands while working. Cut the dough in two parts. Place one of the pieces on the work surface, and flatten it with a rolling pin until it is very thin. Repeat the same steps with the other half of the dough, making a pasta sheet of the same size. Set it aside, covered with a moist towel if necessary to prevent the pasta from drying too much.
- 4) Place about 1 teaspoon of the filling on the dough, spaced 2 inches (5 cm) apart.
- 5) In a skillet large enough to contain the ravioli, place the butter and sage leaves. Turn the heat on just long enough to melt the butter. Bring water to a boil in a stockpot. Gently drop the ravioli in the boiling water a few at a time
- 6) Cook until the pasta is al dente (firm but not too soft or overcooked). Drain ravioli, picking them from the boiling water with a slotted spoon
- 7) Transfer the ravioli to the pan. Stir gently until they are evenly coated with the butter. Combine the grated cheese. Place in a warm serving dish and serve at once.

83. Ravioli In Pinon Cream Sauce Recipe

Serving: 4 | Prep: | Cook: 20mins | Ready in:

Ingredients

- 1 package (1 lb) meat-stuffed ravioli

- 1 cup pinon nuts
- 1 1/4 cups heavy cream
- 1/2 cup grated parmesan cheese
- 2 Tbsp parsley, finely chopped

Direction

- In a large pot of boiling salted water, cook the ravioli according to package directions just until tender but still firm, about 7 minutes.
- Place the pinons in a food processor and process until they are finely ground.
- Heat the cream in a saucepan. Stir in the ground pinons and Parmesan cheese. Heat through, being careful that the cream doesn't boil.
- When the ravioli are done, drain off the water and pour them into a serving bowl. Pour the sauce over the ravioli and sprinkle on the parsley. Serve immediately.

84. Ravioli With Balsamic Brown Butter Recipe

Serving: 4 | Prep: | Cook: 10mins | Ready in:

Ingredients

- 18 to 20 ounces store-bought ravioli (cheese, mushroom, or squash)
- 6 tablespoons unsalted butter
- 2 tablespoons balsamic vinegar
- 1/2 teaspoon salt
- 1/4 teaspoon freshly ground black pepper
- 1/3 cup toasted, chopped walnuts
- 1/4 cup grated Parmesan
- ~
- NOTE: To be honest, I do not like walnuts, never have. I would use pecans or almonds here. But It does not really matter what you use, it still looks so good!

Direction

- Bring a large pot of salted water to a boil over high heat.
- Add the ravioli and cook 4 to 5 minutes, until tender but still firm to the bite, stirring occasionally.
- Drain ravioli onto a large serving platter.
- Meanwhile, in a medium saucepan cook the butter over medium heat, stirring occasionally.
- When the foam subsides, and the butter begins to turn a golden brown, about 3 minutes, turn off the heat.
- Let cool for about 1 minute.
- Stir in the balsamic vinegar, salt, and pepper.
- Transfer the ravioli to the pan saucepan with the balsamic brown butter. Sprinkle walnuts and Parmesan over the top.
- Serve immediately.

85. Ravioli With Corn Recipe

Serving: 6 | Prep: | Cook: 15mins | Ready in:

Ingredients

- 2 (9 oz.) pkgs. refrigerated cheese ravioli
- 3 Tbsp. olive oil
- 3 garlic cloves, minced
- 2 (11 oz.) cans corn with red and green peppers
- 1 cup chopped tomato
- 1/4 cup grated parmesan cheese

Direction

- In large pot of boiling water, cook ravioli according to package directions and drain well.
- Meanwhile, while pasta is cooking, heat oil in large skillet and sauté garlic for 2-3 minutes, stirring constantly. Drain corn well and add to garlic; cook and stir until hot. Add ravioli and toss to coat well. Sprinkle with cheese and serve

86. Ravioli With Northwest Pesto Sauce Recipe

Serving: 8 | Prep: | Cook: 20mins | Ready in:

Ingredients

- two pillow packs of fresh chicken or cheese ravioli
- small jar pesto sauce
- one small sweet onion, sliced thin
- one small granny smith apple - sliced thin and diced
- 1/4 cup walnuts, chopped
- 5 oz pkg crumbled gorgonzola
- salt & pepper to taste

Direction

- In stock pot, boil the ravioli to get it ready to be tossed with the pesto sauce in sauté pan.
- In sauté pan over medium heat, add some olive oil and the onions. Season with salt & pepper to taste. Cook until onions are turning translucent and slightly browning
- Add the granny smith apple and walnuts, cook a few more minutes and add the pesto sauce. Stir together.
- Drain the ravioli and add to the sauté pan. Gently stir together until the pesto sauce evenly coats the ravioli.
- Dish the ravioli and sprinkle with some crumbled gorgonzola before serving.

87. Ravioli With Nutty Cream Sauce Recipe

Serving: 4 | Prep: | Cook: 10mins | Ready in:

Ingredients

- 12 oz frozen or fresh ravioli or tortellini
- 1/3 cup finely chopped pine nuts
- 1/4 cup finely chopped hazelnuts
- 2 tbsp. finely chopped walnuts
- 3/4 cup whipping cream
- 2 tbsp. butter
- salt and pepper to taste
- 1/4 cup grated parmesan cheese

Direction

- In a large pot of boiling salted water cook ravioli according to package directions or until al dente; drain.
- In a bowl combine pine nuts, hazelnuts and walnuts,
- In a large saucepan, combine cream, butter and half the nut mixture; bring to a boil. Stir in pasta; season to taste with salt and pepper. Serve immediately, sprinkled with remaining nuts and Parmesan cheese.

88. Ravioli With Oil And Garlic Recipe

Serving: 4 | Prep: | Cook: 10mins | Ready in:

Ingredients

- 1 package frozen cheese ravioli
- 1/2 cup extra virgin olive oil
- 3 cloves garlic, finely minced
- 1 tsp. dried parsley
- 1 tsp. dried basil
- 1/2 tsp. salt
- 1 Tbs. fresh lemon juice
- 4 Tbs. butter (not margarine)
- 2 Tbs. freshley grated parmesan cheese

Direction

- Prepare frozen ravioli as directed on package.
- Meanwhile for sauce, place olive oil and garlic in a small saucepan and cook over medium heat until garlic is soft. Stir in basil, parsley, lemon juice, salt and butter.

- Drain ravioli well and place in a large shallow serving dish. Sprinkle with cheese and pour hot sauce over all. Gently toss until well coated.
- Serve immediately passing around extra cheese for individual use.

89. Ravioli With Roasted Squash And Sage Brown Butter Recipe

Serving: 6 | Prep: | Cook: 35mins | Ready in:

Ingredients

- 1 1/2 pounds butternut squash, peeled and diced into into 1/2-inch pieces
- 1 tablespoon olive oil
- 30 (about 2 1/2 pounds) frozen jumbo 4-cheese ravioli
- 1 stick unsalted butter
- 1/3 onion, minced
- 24 small whole sage leaves
- 1/2 cup grated parmesan cheese
- 1/4 teaspoon salt
- 1/4 teaspoon ground black pepper

Direction

- Heat oven to 475 degrees F. Toss squash with oil on a baking sheet with sides; spread in an even layer. Roast 25 minutes, tossing once or twice, or until browned on edges and tender. While squash roasts, bring a large pot of salted water to a boil.
- Five minutes before squash is cooked, add frozen ravioli to boiling water and cook 3 to 5 minutes or according to package directions, until tender. Scoop the ravioli out of the water with a large slotted spoon to a colander and drain well.
- While pasta is cooking, melt butter in a skillet over low to medium heat. Add onion and cook 3 minutes, then add sage leaves and slowly cook until butter is golden brown and smells nutty, and sage leaves are crisp. Watch carefully, as it will change from golden to burned very quickly.
- To serve, arrange 5 ravioli on each plate and top with roasted squash and Parmesan. Spoon brown butter and sage leaves over each serving and season with salt and pepper.

90. Raviolis Stuffed With Beemster XO Recipe

Serving: 24 | Prep: | Cook: 5mins | Ready in:

Ingredients

- 1 cup coarsely grated Beemster® XO and Beemster with herbs
- 1 tablespoon parsley, finely chopped
- 1 tablespoon chives, finely chopped
- 1 tablespoon basil, finely chopped
- 2 egg yolks
- Pinch of nutmeg
- 2 cups fresh pasta dough
- 1 cup cream
- Freshly ground pepper

Direction

- To make the filling, combine the grated cheese and parsley, chives, basil, egg yolks, nutmeg and freshly ground pepper.
- Roll out the pasta dough on a worktop that has been lightly dusted with flour until it is around 1/8 inch thick.
- Cut the dough into two sheets of equal size and place spoonfuls of the filling on one sheet every 2 inches.
- Cover with the other sheet and press down gently with your fingers around each spoonful of filling to create the raviolis.
- Cut out the raviolis using a round shape (or other fun shape), press down on them once again (primarily to squeeze out the air bubbles) and place them on a clean dishtowel.
- Boil the raviolis for 4 to 5 minutes and drain.
- Add the cream and heat gently.

- Sprinkle with chives and serve on warm plates

91. Ravoli With Fresh Sage Butter Recipe

Serving: 4 | Prep: | Cook: | Ready in:

Ingredients

- 3 bunches fresh sage
- 8 tbsp unsalted butter
- 1 lb fresh ravioli
- Salt & pepper to taste

Direction

- Julienne 6 or so sage leaves. Put aside. Chop enough sage to pack 1/2 cup.
- Bring a large pot of water to a boil, Salt the water. Add ravioli and cook until al dente.
- Melt about 6 tbsp. butter in a large skillet. Add chopped sage, salt & pepper to taste. Cook over medium heat until butter just begins to brown & bubble, sage should be crispy.
- Drain ravioli, save 1/4 cup cooking water. Immediately put pasta in a warm bowl, add remaining butter. Toss with melted butter & sage mixture and add enough cooking water to make a sauce. Salt & pepper to taste, sprinkle with julienned sage. Enjoy!

92. Roasted Butternut Squash Ravioli Recipe

Serving: 4 | Prep: | Cook: 3mins | Ready in:

Ingredients

- 1 butternut squash
- 1.5 Tbsp. of sage
- 1 shallot, finely chopped
- 1 medium onion, finely chopped
- 1 tbsp of olive oil
- salt and pepper
- 1 lb of Fresh pasta Dough (see my recipe for 'Homemade pasta'

Direction

- Preheat oven to 400 degrees.
- Wash and Cut the Squash in half lengthwise
- Roast the squash face down for about One hour and fifteen minutes, allow to cool.
- Meanwhile, heat oil in pan and add onion, shallot and sage, cooking for about 5-7 minutes until onions are tender.
- If the onions are too chunky - chop in food processor, then set aside.
- Scoop squash from skins with a spoon, and mash in a large bowl.
- Then add the onion mixture and salt and pepper.
- Divide the dough into 8 pieces. Roll each piece through pasta machine as directed, until it is at its thinnest setting.
- With each piece of dough, place rounded teaspoons of filling 3/4 of an inch apart down one side of the dough - then fold it over and carefully seal each ravioli, getting all the air out. Cut immediately into individual pieces and place on floured surface to rest/dry for 10-30 minutes.
- Refrigerate for up to 24 hours, or freeze to use later.
- Take a deep breath, relax - and then enjoy your hard work!

93. Roasted Winter Squash Ravioli With Sausage Cream Sauce Recipe

Serving: 4 | Prep: | Cook: 30mins | Ready in:

Ingredients

- Filling:
- 3 TBS minced onion

- 2 cup roasted squash puree (or canned puree)
- 6 Tablespoons heavy cream
- 6 Tablespoons grated parmigiano-reggiano cheese
- Pinch nutmeg
- salt and pepper
- Sauce:
- 1 Tablespoon olive oil
- 1/2 lb sweet Italian sausage
- 2 cloves garlic, minced
- 1/2 onion, finely chopped
- 1 teaspoon dried sage
- 1 cup dry white wine
- 1 cup chicken stock
- 1/4 - 1/2 cup of heavy cream
- 1/8 teaspoon cinnamon
- 1/2 teaspoon nutmeg
- salt and pepper
- One recipe of pasta dough, rolled out to 1/4 inch thickness

Direction

- In a large sauté pan, over medium heat, melt 1 TBS of butter. Add the squash puree and cook until the mixture is slightly dry, about 2 to 3 minutes. Season with salt and pepper. Stir in the cream and continue to cook for 2 minutes. Remove from heat and stir in 6 TBS cheese and nutmeg to taste. Cool Completely.
- Make an egg wash by whisking 1 egg and 1 teaspoon of water and set aside in a small bowl.
- Cut the pasta into desired shape (round or square) about 3 inches in diameter. Place 1 - 2 teaspoons of the filling in the center of pasta shape. Wet the edges with egg wash and top with the other pasta shape to seal, making sure there are no air bubbles. I work in batches because it's easier.
- Add Ravioli to a pot of boiling salted water. Cook until al dente, about 2 to 3 minutes or until the pasta floats and is pale in color. Work in batches. . .
- Remove the pasta from water and drain well, Season with salt and pepper. Set aside to make the sauce.
- Sauce: Heat skillet over medium high heat. Add 1 tablespoon of olive oil to the pan and brown the sausage. Add garlic and onion, sauté until onions are translucent.
- Add sage, wine, reduce wine to half. Add stock and stir in the cream. Season the sauce with cinnamon and nutmeg, salt and pepper to taste. Simmer the sauce to desired thickness.
- Add the Ravioli and toss for a minute. Garnish with Parmesan Cheese.

94. SEAFOOD STUFFED RAVIOLI Recipe

Serving: 4 | Prep: | Cook: 15mins | Ready in:

Ingredients

- 1/4 cup dinely chopped shrimp
- 1/4 cup finely chopped crab meat
- 3/4 cup shredded old cheddar cheese
- 24 wonton wrappers
- 2 tbsp butter
- 1 cup chopped leeks, (white & light green part only
- 1 tbsp finely grated lime zest
- 3/4 cup 35% whipping cream
- 1/4 cup shicken stock
- 2 tbsp freshly squeezed lime juice
- Salt & pepper
- 1/4 cup parmesan cheese
- 1/4 cup chopped chives

Direction

- In a bowl combine shrimp, crab and cheese.
- Place half the wonton wrappers on work surface.
- Place 2 tbsp. of seafood mixture in centre of each.
- Brush water around edges of wrapper; top with second wrapper. Press together; pressing out air and sealing edges.
- Place on parchment lined baking sheet.
- Lime Cream Sauce:

- In medium skillet, melt butter over medium-high heat until browned and bubbly, but not burnt.
- Add leeks and lime zest; sauté for about 3 min or until leeks start to soften.
- Add cream, stock and lime juice; cook stirring occasionally for about 2 min or until sauce comes to boil.
- Remove from heat and season to taste with salt and pepper. In large wide pot of boiling water.
- Cook ravioli, for about 3 to 5 min or until tender.
- Remove with a slotted spoon; transfer to shallow bowls.
- Spoon lime cream sauce over ravioli; sprinkle with Parmesan and chives.

95. SPINACH RAVIOLI LASAGNA Recipe

Serving: 6 | Prep: | Cook: 45mins | Ready in:

Ingredients

- Ingredients:
- 1 26-oz Jar of italian tomato sauce
- 2 Packages of Frozen Mama Rosie's cheese and spinach ravioli, unthawed(or equivalent)
- 1 package of frozen chopped spinach thawed and squeezed dry
- 1 8-oz package of shredded part-skim mozzarella cheese
- ½ cup grated parmesan cheese
- Non-stick cooking spray

Direction

- 1) Preheat oven to 375
- 2) 13" x 9" baking dish sprayed with non-stick cooking spray
- 3) Spread a layer of sauce and grated cheese on the bottom of the baking dish, then a layer of ravioli over the sauce covering the bottom. Then sprinkle a layer of spinach over the raviolis, then mozzarella, then sauce, then grated cheese. Continue ending with ravioli, sauce, and mozzarella cheese.
- 4) Cover with foil and bake for 30 minutes. Uncover and bake for 10 minutes or until bubbly.
- 5) Let cool for only 5 minutes before serving.
- Serving size is 1/6 of the recipe.
- Calories per serving: 350, Carbohydrate: 45g, Fat: 14g, Sodium: 260mg, Cholesterol: 100mg

96. Sausage And Ravioli In Garlic And Olive Oil Recipe

Serving: 2 | Prep: | Cook: 1hours | Ready in:

Ingredients

- Frozen ravioli, 5 per person
- 1 onion, sliced
- 1 pepper, sliced
- salt and pepper to taste
- 2 italian sausage
- olive oil to fry
- parmesan cheese, grated
- olive oil and garlic sauce
- 1/2 cup extra virgin olive oil
- 2 tbls. garlic, chopped
- Pinch red pepper flakes
- salt to taste

Direction

- Put large pot of water on to boil
- In fry pan, pour 3/4 cup water and bring to simmer
- Add sausage and cook on both sides are browned through
- Remove water from pan and add a little oil
- Cook over medium heat to brown all sides
- Set aside
- In large fry pan over med heat, add olive oil, peppers, onions, salt and pepper
- Sauté until tender crisp

- Lower heat to low
- Add garlic, olive oil, red pepper flakes and salt
- Stir to combine
- Slice sausage to your liking
- Add to pepper mixture
- Cook ravioli according to package directions
- Add to sausage mixture
- Sprinkle with Parmesan cheese before serving

97. Seafood Ravioli With White Wine Sauce Recipe

Serving: 8 | Prep: | Cook: 10mins | Ready in:

Ingredients

- white wine Sauce:
- 2 tbsp olive oil
- ½ cup chopped onion
- 1 clove garlic, crushed
- 2 tbsp white all-purpose flour
- ¾ bottle light white wine (riesling or sauvignon blanc)
- 1 x 8oz can clam nectar
- 1 x 8oz can undiluted chicken stock
- Reserved liquid from raw scallops
- 1 tbsp dried oregano
- 1 tbsp chopped parsley
- salt and pepper to taste
- Filling:
- 8oz raw bay scallops (reserve liquid)
- 2 tbsp olive oil
- ¼ cup chopped onion
- 1 clove garlic, crushed
- ½ cup cooked and drained chopped spinach
- ¼ cup ricotta cheese
- ¼ cup blue cheese, crumbled
- ¼ cup soft goat or sheep cheese
- 1 tbsp. chopped parsley
- ¼ cup smoked salmon
- salt and pepper to taste
- Ravioli:
- 3 cups white all-purpose flour
- 3 eggs, lightly beaten
- 1 tbsp. vegetable oil

Direction

- White Wine Sauce:
- In a large skillet heat the olive oil over medium-high then add the onions and garlic. When the onions begin to brown, add the flour and stir for one minute. Add the wine and stir until smooth. Reduce until the mixture is thick, then thin with the clam nectar, reserved scallop liquid, and chicken stock as necessary until the consistency coats the back of a spoon. Add the oregano and parsley and simmer lightly while the ravioli is being prepared.
- Filling:
- Drain the raw scallops and reserve the liquid. In a large skillet heat the olive oil over medium-high then add the onions and garlic. When the onions begin to brown, turn the heat to high then add the scallops. When the scallops are browned slightly, remove from the heat and combine with the rest of the filling ingredients. Pulse the mixture in a food processor until smooth.
- Ravioli:
- In a large bowl add the eggs to the flour, then add the oil. Move to a lightly floured surface and knead for 3 minutes. The dough should be smooth and elastic, not sticky. Add another egg if it is too dry. Divide in half and let stand for 30 minutes under a damp cloth.
- Prepare the filling.
- Divide the 2 dough portions into quarters. Run the dough through the pasta maker on the largest setting 4 times, folding the dough over itself each time. Run the dough through subsequent smaller settings, stretching the dough each time as required to ensure it is the maximum width of the pasta machine rollers. Dust lightly with flour between each rolling. Once the dough is about 16" long and 1/16 inch thick you are done. Place under cloth and make another. Use a tablespoon measure and place the fillings on the dough, flat side down, in a grid of about 2 x 8 portions, with at least an inch between portions. Brush between the

portions with water. Lay the second dough on top. Form the dough around the portions, eliminating the air pockets as much as possible, then seal the edges. Cut the ravioli with a knife or a ravioli cutter. Boil in a large pot of salted water for 5 – 8 minutes, drain and serve topped with the white wine sauce. Garnish with freshly chopped parsley.

98. Seared Scallops Mango Ravioli Prosciutto Parsnip Chips Balsamic Pomegranate Reduction Recipe

Serving: 1 | Prep: | Cook: 20mins | Ready in:

Ingredients

- 250 g water
- 1.3 g Sodium Citrate
- 1.8 g Sodium Alginate
- 250 g mango Puree
- 1000 g water
- 5 g Calcium Chloride
- 5 each scallops
- 1 parsnip, shaved thinly on a mandoline into chips
- 1 oz prosciutto, julienned
- 2 oz balsamic vinegar
- 1 t pomegranate molasses

Direction

- For Mango Ravioli
- Make a setting bath by blending the calcium chloride with the 1000g of water using an immersion blender until totally dissolved. Set aside to allow the air bubbles to escape.
- Blend the sodium citrate with the 250 g of water, add the sodium alginate and blend once more with an immersion blender. Bring mixture to a boil, remove from heat and allow to cool. Mix in the mango puree.
- Using a spoon, scoop the mango mixture and drop it into the calcium chloride bath to form spheres. Allow to set in the bath for 2 minutes. Remove and rinse in a water bath. (Do this last step no longer than 5-7 minutes before you plate up your dish as the ravioli will deteriorate in quality.
- For Balsamic and Pomegranate Molasses
- Place the balsamic vinegar and pomegranate molasses in a small sauce pan and bring to a simmer over high heat whisking until you emulsify them together. Remove from heat and reserve.
- For the Parsnip Chips and Prosciutto
- Fry the chips and the prosciutto separately until crispy. For the chips, remove from fryer, place on paper towels to remove excess oil, season with salt. For the prosciutto, mince into fine pieces and reserve.
- For Scallops
- Pat scallops dry to remove excess moisture and season with salt and pepper. Sear in a scorching hot sauté pan with a small amount of oil.
- To Plate
- Place mango ravioli on plate, arrange one parsnip chip with each ravioli. Place scallops around plate and drizzle with balsamic pomegranate reduction. Sprinkle the finely diced prosciutto around the dish.

99. Shiitake Pumpkin Ravioli Recipe

Serving: 4 | Prep: | Cook: 20mins | Ready in:

Ingredients

- 1 tablespoon extra virgin olive oil
- 16 shitake mushrooms, stemmed and finely diced
- 1/2 cup onion, minced
- 1 clove garlic, minced
- 4 tsp grated fresh ginger

- 1 teaspoon low-sodium soy sauce
- 1 1/2 cups canned pumpkin puree
- 1/4 cup toasted sesame seeds
- 1/3 cup shredded zucchini
- 1/2 cup low-fat silken tofu, mashed or pureed
- 2 tbsp dry whole-wheat breadcrumbs
- 1 tsp fresh ground pepper
- 48 square wonton wrappers

Direction

- In large pan, heat olive oil.
- Add mushrooms, onion, garlic and ginger.
- Cook over medium-low heat for approximately 7-8 minutes or until tender.
- Stir in the soy sauce, then raise heat to high.
- Cook, stirring constantly, 5 minutes.
- Transfer to a large bowl and let cool slightly.
- Stir in pumpkin puree, sesame seeds, zucchini, tofu and bread crumbs. Add pepper and fold in well.
- Working in small batches, spoon 1 teaspoon of filling slightly off-center of each wonton wrapper (keep remaining wontons under a damp towel).
- Brush edges with water and fold over to form a triangle. Press edges together firmly (I use a fork) to seal.
- Wrap well, and refrigerate for 1-24 hours before cooking, or lay onto a baking sheet and freeze before transferring to a bag for storage (they will keep in the freezer about 3 months).
- Bring a large pot of salted water to a boil.
- Reduce the heat to a simmer and lower the ravioli into the pot.
- Cook until they float to the surface, about 4 - 5 minutes.
- Remove with slotted spoon and drain well.
- Serve with any sauce of your choice, or plain.

100. Sicilian Ricotta Ravioli Filling Recipe

Serving: 4 | Prep: | Cook: 5mins | Ready in:

Ingredients

- 1.5 cups ricotta cheese
- 1 cup coarsely grated parmesan cheese
- 1-2 cups of wilted, chopped, fresh spinach
- 3 tbs pine nuts
- 3 tbs sultanas, chopped
- nutmeg to taste

Direction

- Mix all the ingredients. It's best to do this by hand -- a food processor will chop the pine nuts and you'll want them whole.
- Put 1 tbsp. of filling in each ravioli.
- (For a recipe for the pasta dough and ravioli procedure, try this: Pumpkin Ravioli)

101. Simone Remoli's Father's Day Meaty Treat: Oxtail Ravioli Recipe

Serving: 4 | Prep: | Cook: 30mins | Ready in:

Ingredients

- \- 1 full oxtail (2kgs)
- \- 2 carrots
- \- 1 head of celery
- \- 1 onion
- \- 1 bay leaf and 1 stick of majoram
- \- 4 fresh tomatoes chopped
- \- 500ml full-bodied red wine
- \- 3 cloves, 1 star anise
- \- Salt and pepper
- \- Water as required
- \- Olive oil
- \- Fresh pasta sheets

Direction

- 1. Rinse the tail, dry and cut into chunks, or drums
- 2. Chop the carrots, celery and onion into fairly large chunks. Put in a large deep pan

with the olive oil, bay leaf, marjoram, cloves, star anise and chopped tomatoes. Sweat for 15-20 minutes over a medium heat and put aside.

- 3. In the same pan brown the tail for at least 10-15 minutes on all sides. Add salt and pepper to release the water from the meat and then add the wine. At this point you will hear what I call, 'The Sound of Kitchen Heaven'! The point when the wine hits the boiling pan. Now scrape off any meat juices at the bottom of the pan.
- 4. Put the braised vegetables back in the pan along with enough water to completely cover the meat. Bring to boil and then put it in the oven for at least three hours at 190°c grade, always making sure the meat is covered, adding boiling water if necessary. When the meat easily falls away from the bone it is ready. Note that this could take longer than 3 hours.
- 5. When you have finished cooking, take the tail out of the sauce and put it in a container, cover with cling film and wait for it to cool down.
- 6. In the meantime remove the bay leaf and the marjoram stick from the sauce and blend until smooth and creamy. Add salt and pepper to taste.
- 7. Remove the meat from the bone and smash it with your hands until it reaches a homogeneous texture ready to fill our fresh pasta.
- 8. Fill the pasta sheets with the oxtail filling and prepare the ravioli.
- 9. Cook the pasta for three minutes and serve in the oxtail sauce. Top with a drizzle of olive oil and pecorino cheese.

102. Slow Cooker Cheesy Ravioli Casserole Recipe

Serving: 12 | Prep: | Cook: 300mins | Ready in:

Ingredients

- 1 tablespoon olive or vegetable oil
- 1 medium onion, chopped (1/2 cup)
- 1 large clove garlic, finely chopped
- 1 can (26 ounces) four cheese-flavored spaghetti sauce
- 1 can (15 ounces) tomato sauce
- 1 teaspoon italian seasoning
- 2 packages (25 ounces each) frozen beef-filled ravioli
- 2 cups shredded mozzarella cheese (8 ounces)
- 1/4 cup chopped fresh parsley

Direction

- In 10-inch skillet, heat oil over medium heat. Cook onion and garlic in oil about 4 minutes, stirring occasionally, until onion is tender. Stir in spaghetti sauce, tomato sauce and Italian seasoning.
- Place 1 cup of the sauce mixture in bottom of 5- to 6-quart slow cooker. Add 1 package frozen ravioli; top with 1 cup of the cheese. Top with remaining package of ravioli; top with remaining 1 cup cheese. Pour remaining sauce mixture over top.
- Cover and cook on low heat setting 5 to 7 hours or until ravioli are tender. Sprinkle with parsley.

103. Slow Cooker Ravioli Lasagna Recipe

Serving: 0 | Prep: | Cook: 6hours | Ready in:

Ingredients

- 1 lb. ground beef
- 1 cup chopped onion (one medium onion)
- 2 garlic cloves, finely chopped
- 1 jar (24 oz) tomato pasta sauce of your choice
- 1 pkg (26 oz) frozen cheese-filled ravioli (do not thaw)
- 2 cups shredded cheese - Italian, mozzarella or a blend

Direction

- Spray 3-1/2 to 4 quart slow cooker with cooking spray. In skillet, cook beef, onion and garlic until beef is thoroughly cooked; drain.
- Spoon 3/4 cup of the pasta sauce in bottom of slow cooker. Layer half of the ravioli, half of the beef mixture and 1 cup of the cheese over sauce. Repeat layers with 3/4 cup sauce, remaining ravioli and remaining beef mixture. Top with remaining sauce; sprinkle with remaining 1 cup cheese.
- Cover; cook on low heat setting 6 hours or until ravioli is tender.
- My notes: to half this, I used 1/2 lb. of ground beef, 1/2 cup of onion and 1 garlic clove. I used 1-1/2 cups of a garlic and onion pasta sauce. I had one package (16 oz.) of beef/spinach ravioli. I used 1 cup of mozzarella.
- I think this may get done in 5 hours. It probably depends on the slow cooker but I think mine would have been done in 5 hours. I would recommend checking your ravioli in 5 hours.

104. Smoked Salmon Ravioli Recipe

Serving: 4 | Prep: | Cook: 6mins | Ready in:

Ingredients

- • 2 cups all-purpose flour
- • 2 eggs, beaten
- • 2 egg yolks
- • 1 pound smoked salmon
- • 2 eggs
- • 1 cup heavy cream
- • 2 teaspoons chopped fresh chives
- • 1/2 teaspoon ground black pepper
- • 1 egg, beaten
- • 16 ounces shredded gruyere cheese
- • 1 cup heavy whipping cream

Direction

- 1. TO MAKE THE PASTA, place the flour in a mound on a smooth work area, creating a well in the center. Pour the 2 beaten eggs and 2 egg yolks into the well, and slowly pull the flour into the eggs until it is all incorporated. Finish kneading by hand, adding more flour if needed for a smooth consistency. Divide the pasta in half and roll out each half or feed through pasta roller until thin, number 6 setting on the machine. Roll out as many sheets of pasta as possible.
- 2. FOR THE SMOKED SALMON MOUSSE, puree the smoked salmon and 2 eggs together until smooth. Slowly add 1 cup heavy cream, chopped chives, and pepper. Mix thoroughly.
- 3. To assemble the raviolis, prepare a smooth, floured surface. Lay out the pasta and divide the smoked salmon mousse into 24 equal-sized portions and place these portions two inches apart on one sheet of pasta. Brush the beaten egg on the pasta between the mounds of salmon mousse, and cover with the other sheet of pasta. Cut raviolis apart, and refrigerate or freeze until you are ready to use.
- 4. Bring a large pot of lightly salted water to a boil, add raviolis, and cook about 6 minutes. Drain well.
- 5. Meanwhile, add to each of 8 fireproof plates 1 ounce gruyere cheese and 1/8 cup heavy cream. Heat under the broiler until the cheese melts then adds the raviolis and sprinkle 1 ounce more gruyere on top. Place under the broiler until the cheese browns lightly.
- 6. Serve the stuffed raviolis on the warm plates.

105. Speedy Chicken And Ravioli Recipe

Serving: 4 | Prep: | Cook: 20mins | Ready in:

Ingredients

- vegetable cooking spray
- 1 pound chicken tenders cut into 1/2" pieces
- 3/4 cup chopped white onion
- 2 teaspoons minced garlic
- 3/4 cup canned kidney beans rinsed and drained
- 1 large tomato cubed
- 1/2 teaspoon dried thyme leaves
- 9 ounces fresh sun dried tomato ravioli cooked
- 1/4 teaspoon salt
- 1/2 teaspoon freshly ground black pepper

Direction

- Spray large skillet with cooking spray then heat over medium heat until hot.
- Cook chicken, onion and garlic until browned about 8 minutes.
- Stir in beans, tomato and thyme then cook 3 minutes and stir in ravioli.
- Cook 2 minutes more and season with salt and pepper then serve immediately.

106. Spicy Beef And Sausage Ravioli With Ariabatta Sauce Recipe

Serving: 2 | Prep: | Cook: 1mins | Ready in:

Ingredients

- Buitoni Spicy beef & sausage Ravioli (in the deli section)
- Trader Joe's Sauce Arabiatta

Direction

- If you've ever made ravioli you probably don't need directions for it but here it goes. Just get some water to boil and put in 6 raviolis in per person. The package makes enough for 2 or one really hungry person-like ME! It takes about 8 minutes or so to cook them. I put the timer in the kitchen on for 10 minutes and then just remove slightly before if needed.
- Heat the sauce up and then spoon over the cooked ravioli.
- I wouldn't recommend this sauce for kids as it has kind of a zip to it-spicy, that is.
- Another sauce that is great with this dish and goes with the spicy sausage and beef flavor in the ravioli is pesto genovese. I used some Trader Joe's bottled Pesto. You'll find it in a very small jar and a little goes a long way.
- You can make what I call a 50/50 Plate by coating 3 of the ravioli with the Arrabbiata sauce and then the other 3 with some Pesto and serve to a willing participant.
- Tell me how you like it and also any adaptions you make on the dish and I'll include them here to share with others and also in my upcoming cookbook.
- God bless and happy cooking to all who have read this or made it.

107. Spicy Spinach And Cheese Ravioli Recipe

Serving: 4 | Prep: | Cook: 1hours | Ready in:

Ingredients

- 3/4 cup non-fat cottage cheese, well drained
- 1 tbsp chickpea flour
- 1/2 tsp lemon juice
- 1/4 cup rice Parmesan (or low-fat Parmesan)
- 1/2 tsp kosher salt
- 1/2 tsp lemon pepper
- 1/4 tsp cayenne pepper
- 1 clove garlic, crushed
- 5 oz (1/2 a box) frozen chopped spinach, thawed and squeezed dry
- 32 gyoza wrappers (the round ones)

Direction

- In a food processor or blender, combine cottage cheese, chickpea flour, lemon juice, rice Parmesan, salt, lemon pepper, cayenne and garlic.

- Puree until smooth and pour into a bowl.
- Fold in the spinach until well incorporated.
- Fill the centre of each gyoza wrapper with 1 tsp. of the filling, then seal by wetting the edges of the wrapper and folding into a half-moon shape.
- Cover and refrigerate 30 minutes.
- Cook ravioli in boiling, salted water for 3-4 minutes. Serve with a light tomato or pesto sauce.

108. Spinach And Ravioli Recipe

Serving: 2 | Prep: | Cook: 35mins | Ready in:

Ingredients

- 3 T. olive oil
- 1 medium red onion, peeled and sliced
- salt and pepper
- 5 cloves fresh crushed garlic
- 1 small portabello mushroom, sliced thin and cut into small pieces
- 12-16 oz. fresh baby spinach
- 1 t. balsamic vinegar
- 1 10 oz. package tofu and roasted red pepper Ravioli
- 1 additional tablespoon olive oil
- 1 T. grated Locatelli cheese
- 1-2 T. crumbled Chevre (goat) cheese
- .

Direction

- Heat the oil in a large sauté pan over a medium high flame. Add the onions, season with some salt and pepper and begin to sauté. When the onions take on some light brown color, add the garlic, then the mushroom slices, toss and continue to cook.
- Heat the oil in a large sauté pan over a medium high flame.
- Add the onions, season with some salt and pepper and begin to sauté.
- When the onions take on some light brown color, add the garlic, then the mushroom slices, toss and continue to cook.
- Bring about 3 quarts of water to a boil and cook the ravioli. Meanwhile, add the spinach to the sauté pan and toss using tongs to combine the ingredients.
- Pour in the balsamic vinegar, toss and simmer just until the spinach is well wilted.
- When the ravioli are cooked, drain them, then toss with the additional olive oil and the grated cheese.
- To serve, divide the spinach sauté onto two serving plates.
- Top with the ravioli and garnish with the crumbled goat cheese. Serve immediately.

109. Spinach Garlic Ravioli Recipe

Serving: 46 | Prep: | Cook: 15mins | Ready in:

Ingredients

- 1/2 Frozen ravioli of your choice (I like mushroom)
- 1/2 Boxed spinach (defrosted & water squeezed out)
- 4-6 garlic cloves, chopped
- extra virgin olive oil (to heavily coat pan)
- butter (about 1/4 of a stick)
- heavy cream (about 1/4 to 1/3 cup)
- dried basil
- salt & pepper to taste
- parmesan cheese
- (sorry, I don't usually measure when I cook)

Direction

- Defrost spinach in microwave for about 1 minute. Squeeze out water & set aside
- Boil frozen ravioli until it floats to the top
- Chop garlic cloves, set aside
- Coat pan with olive oil, melt butter in pan with oil

- Add chopped garlic, sprinkle of basil, salt & pepper
- Cook a couple of minutes until garlic soft
- Add cooked ravioli and mix so it gets covered with garlic sauce
- Add spinach, cream & sprinkle with parmesan cheese, stir and cook about another 2 minutes or so
- Add more salt & pepper to taste & serve
- Top with more parmesan if desired
- (Sorry I don't really have good measurements. This is my first recipe here. I just made this yesterday for dinner & loved it, so I thought I'd add it here. Hope you like it.)

110. Spinach Ravioli Recipe

Serving: 6 | Prep: | Cook: 10mins | Ready in:

Ingredients

- 48 egg-free pot sticker skins
- 1 cup tomatoes — peeled, seeded and diced
- 1 small onion — oven roasted
- 1 cup mushrooms — minced
- 2 teaspoons garlic — minced
- 1/2 pound spinach leaves — blanched, chopped
- 1/4 cup nonfat cottage cheese
- 3/4 cup tofu — mashed
- 2 tablespoons fresh basil — minced
- freshly ground black pepper
- salt — to taste

Direction

- In a large saucepan, combine the tomatoes, onion, mushrooms and garlic. Cook over medium heat until the liquid from the mushrooms completely evaporates and the mixture is somewhat dry. Be careful not to burn it. Set aside to cool.
- In a large bowl, combine the tomato mixture, spinach, cottage cheese, tofu, and basil. Season to taste with pepper and salt.
- On a cutting board, lay out a single layer of pot-sticker skins. Using a pastry brush, moisten the edges with water. Place 1 tablespoon of the spinach mixture onto the center of each skin. Cover with a second potsticker skin and press the edges together with the tines of a fork to seal.
- Cook the ravioli in boiling water or vegetable stock for 3 minutes, or until the potsticker skin is al dente. Serve hot.

111. Sweet Potato Ravioli With Lemon Sage Brown Butter Recipe

Serving: 8 | Prep: | Cook: 60mins | Ready in:

Ingredients

- 1 (1-pound) sweet potato
- 2 tablespoons grated fresh parmesan cheese
- 1/2 teaspoon salt, divided
- 1/4 teaspoon ground cinnamon
- 1/8 teaspoon ground nutmeg
- 24 wonton wrappers
- 1 large egg white, lightly beaten
- 6 quarts water
- cooking spray
- 3 tablespoons butter
- 1 tablespoon chopped fresh sage
- 1 tablespoon fresh lemon juice
- 1/8 teaspoon freshly ground black pepper
- sage sprigs (optional)

Direction

- Preheat oven to 400°.
- Pierce potato several times with a fork; place on a foil-lined baking sheet. Bake at 400° for 40 minutes or until tender. Cool. Peel potato; mash. Combine potato, cheese, 1/4 teaspoon salt, cinnamon, and nutmeg in a small bowl.
- Working with 1 wonton wrapper at a time (cover remaining wrappers with a damp towel

to keep them from drying), spoon 1 tablespoon potato mixture into center of each wrapper. Brush edges of dough with egg white; bring 2 opposite corners to center. Press edges together to seal, forming a triangle. Repeat procedure with remaining wonton wrappers, potato filling, and egg white.
- Bring 6 quarts water to a boil. Add 8 ravioli; cook 2 minutes or until done. Remove ravioli from pan with a slotted spoon. Lightly coat cooked wontons with cooking spray; keep warm. Repeat procedure with remaining ravioli.

112. TEX MEX MINI RAVIOLI SOUP Recipe

Serving: 4 | Prep: | Cook: 20mins | Ready in:

Ingredients

- 1 teaspoon vegetable oil
- 1 large onion (for about 1 cup chopped)
- 2 (14 1/2-ounce) cans fat-free chicken broth
- 1 cup bottled salsa, mild or hot
- 1 cup frozen corn kernels
- 1 (9-ounce) package refrigerated cheese mini ravioli
- 1 (15-ounce) can black beans
- reduced-fat sour cream, optional garnish

Direction

- In a 4 1/2-quart Dutch oven or soup pot, heat the oil over medium heat. Peel and coarsely chop the onion, adding it to the pot as you chop. Stir and cook until the onion starts to soften, about 2 minutes.
- Add the chicken broth, salsa, corn and ravioli to the pot. Raise the heat to high, and bring the soup to a boil.
- Meanwhile, rinse and drain the beans, and add them to the pot. Cook the soup for 5 minutes at a moderate boil, until the ravioli is cooked through and tender. Remove the pot from the heat, and let the soup rest for 5 minutes.
- Ladle the soup into individual serving bowls, and top each serving with a little sour cream, if desired. Serves 4.

113. Taco Ravioli Bake Recipe

Serving: 6 | Prep: | Cook: 33mins | Ready in:

Ingredients

- 2 cans (15 ounce) beef ravioli or 1 large can
- 1 package taco seasoning
- 2/3 cup water
- 1 pound ground beef
- 2 cups shredded cheddar cheese

Direction

- Brown ground beef in skillet. Drain off grease. Add 1 package of taco seasoning mix, 2/3 water and cook for about 8 minutes. Then put ravioli in 9x13 inch casserole dish, add ground beef mixture and all the cheese.
- Bake at 350 for 30 - 35 minutes or until hot and cheese is melted.

114. Toasted Ravioli Puffs

Serving: 4 | Prep: | Cook: 10mins | Ready in:

Ingredients

- 24 refrigerated cheese ravioli
- 1 tablespoon reduced-fat Italian salad dressing
- 1 tablespoon Italian-style panko bread crumbs
- 1 tablespoon grated Parmesan cheese
- Warm marinara sauce

Direction

- Preheat oven to 400°. Cook ravioli according to package directions; drain. Transfer to a greased baking sheet. Brush with salad dressing. In a small bowl, mix bread crumbs and cheese; sprinkle over ravioli.
- Bake 12-15 minutes or until golden brown. Serve with marinara sauce.
- Nutrition Facts
- 1 ravioli: 21 calories, 1g fat (0 saturated fat), 3mg cholesterol, 43mg sodium, 3g carbohydrate (0 sugars, 0 fiber), 1g protein.

115. Tomatoes And Ravioli With Escarole Recipe

Serving: 4 | Prep: | Cook: 20mins | Ready in:

Ingredients

- 1/2 cup chopped white onion
- 2 cloves garlic minced
- 1 tablespoon olive oil
- 3 cups sliced fresh mushrooms
- 2 cups chopped plum tomatoes
- 3/4 cup chicken broth
- 4 cups coarsely chopped escarole
- 1 tablespoon snipped fresh basil
- 1 teaspoon snipped fresh rosemary
- 9 ounce package refrigerated meat filled ravioli
- 1/4 cup pine nuts toasted

Direction

- In a large skillet cook onion and garlic in hot oil 2 minutes.
- Add mushrooms, tomatoes and chicken broth then bring to a boil.
- Reduce heat and simmer uncovered for 7 minutes.
- Add escarole, basil and rosemary stirring just until escarole is wilted.
- Meanwhile cook pasta according to package directions then drain.
- Return pasta to saucepan then pour sauce over pasta and toss to coat.
- Transfer to a warm serving dish and sprinkle with pine nuts.

116. Venison Wonton Ravioli Recipe

Serving: 8 | Prep: | Cook: 30mins | Ready in:

Ingredients

- 2 lb venison burger
- 2 teaspoons oil
- 2 eggs (beaten)
- 1/2 cup parmesan cheese
- 1 teaspoon garlic powder
- 1/2 to 1 teaspoon salt
- 1/2 teaspoon black pepper
- 1/4 cup minced onion
- 1-2 cloves minced garlic
- 1 package of 60 Wonton Wrapers
- 1cup water for dipping fingers in
- canola oil for frying

Direction

- In skillet, heat oil and sauté the onion and garlic
- Add the venison burger and brown
- (Drain any excess fat that remains)
- Remove 1 cup meat mixture and add the parmesan cheese and salt, pepper, garlic powder
- Add eggs a little at a time to the cheese/burger mix to temper then add it all back into skillet and mix well
- Heat through and remove from stove have one cup of water in a bowl to dip fingers in
- Lay out wrappers a couple at a time or whatever seems easiest
- Dip fingers in water and rub the wrapper all over getting every edge
- Spoon about a teaspoon of meat mixture into the middle of a wrapper

- Fold in half
- Push down all around the meat to seal it and set aside
- When you have all your wontons made
- Heat canola oil in heavy pot
- Gently drop a few at a time into oil and cook till golden
- Remove to paper towels to get excess oil
- Serve with favorite marinara to dip in or pour spaghetti sauce over them and add parmesan cheese. Use any sauce your family likes.
- I make 30 at a time and freeze thirty uncooked for later use.

117. White Bean Ravioli With Brown Butter And Caper Sauce Recipe

Serving: 4 | Prep: | Cook: 10mins | Ready in:

Ingredients

- For the ravioli:
- 1 (15-ounce) can cannellini beans
- 1 egg
- 3 tablespoons balsamic vinaigrette
- 1/2 cup freshly grated Parmesan
- 1 teaspoons italian seasoning (recommended: McCormick)
- 24 wonton wrappers (recommended: Dynasty)
- For the sauce:
- 1/2 cup unsalted butter (1 stick)
- 2 tablespoons capers
- 1 teaspoon italian seasoning (recommended: McCormick)
- 1 tablespoon freshly minced parsley leaves
- salt
- Freshly grated Parmesan, for serving

Direction

- For the ravioli:
- In a blender, puree together the beans, egg, vinaigrette, cheese, and Italian seasoning; set aside.
- Working in batches, so the wrappers don't dry out, lay out 6 to 8 wonton wrappers. Place 1/2 tablespoon of bean mixture in the center of each. Moisten 2 connecting edges of the wonton wrapper with your finger dipped in water.
- Fold wrapper in half to form a triangle. Press edges together to seal. Repeat with remaining wonton wrappers and filling.
- Meanwhile, bring a large pot of salted water to a low boil.
- For the sauce:
- Melt butter in a large skillet over medium-high heat. Cook until it begins to brown and have a nutty aroma. Turn off heat and stir in capers and Italian seasoning.
- Working in batches, cook ravioli in boiling salted water until just tender, about 3 minutes. Using slotted spoon, transfer ravioli to hot butter sauce. Add parsley to pan. Use a spoon to coat ravioli with sauce. Transfer to plates and add salt.
- Serve immediately garnished with grated Parmesan
- Note: Make sure your water is gently boiling not a rolling boil or the agitation will cause your ravioli to fall apart.

118. Zesty Cheese Ravioli Recipe

Serving: 2 | Prep: | Cook: 17mins | Ready in:

Ingredients

- ½ c water
- 1 14.5 oz. can no-salt added diced tomatoes, undrained
- or about 5 plum tomatoes diced
- 1 garlic glove or to taste
- 1 (9 ounce) pkg fresh four cheese ravioli

- 2 Cups finely chopped fresh spinach, rib removed or use baby spinach
- 1/8 tsp sugar
- 1/8 tsp pepper
- 1 Tbl grated Parmesan

Direction

- Combine first 3 ingredients in a large saucepan and bring to a boil
- Add Ravioli, cover and cook for 5 minutes, stirring occasionally. Uncover and cook additional 5 minutes or until ravioli is done.
- Stir in spinach, sugar, pepper; cover and cook 2 minutes stirring occasionally. Remove from heat and let stand, covered, 5 minutes.
- Sprinkle each serving with Parmesan
- Yield: 2 servings (2 cups pasta mixture and 1 ½ tsp. cheese)
- Points 6

119. Asparagus Ravioli In Parmesan Broth Recipe

Serving: 6 | Prep: | Cook: 150mins | Ready in:

Ingredients

- pasta dough
- 1 pound asparagus, trimmed
- 5 cups rich chicken stock
- 1 (3-inch) rind from a wedge of parmigiano-Reggiano
- 1 Turkish or 1/2 California bay leaf
- 1/4 cup grated parmigiano-Reggiano
- 1/4 cup mascarpone
- 1/4 cup fine dry bread crumbs
- 1 teaspoon grated lemon zest

Direction

- Make broth and filling while dough stands:
- Cut off asparagus tips, then halve each tip lengthwise and reserve.
- Bring stock, cheese rind, and bay leaf to a simmer in a medium saucepan, then add asparagus stems and cook, uncovered, until stems are just tender, 5 to 6 minutes. Transfer stems to paper towels and cool slightly. Reserve broth.
- Purée asparagus stems in a food processor with grated parmesan, mascarpone, bread crumbs, zest, and 1/2 teaspoon each of salt and pepper.
- Make Ravioli:
- Cut dough into 4 equal pieces. Cover 3 pieces with plastic wrap, then pat out remaining piece into a flat rectangle and generously dust with flour.
- Set rollers of pasta machine on widest setting. Feed rectangle, a short side first, through rollers. Fold rectangle in thirds, like a letter, and feed it, a short side first, through rollers. Repeat 6 or 7 more times, folding dough in thirds and feeding it through rollers, a short side first each time, dusting with flour to prevent sticking.
- Turn dial to next (narrower) setting and feed dough through rollers without folding, a short side first. Continue to feed dough through without folding, making space between rollers narrower each time, until the second- or third-narrowest setting is used. (Do not roll too thin or pasta will tear when filled.)
- Put pasta sheet on a lightly floured kitchen towel (not terry cloth) with a long side nearest you. Drop 6 rounded teaspoon-size mounds of filling 10 inches apart in a row down center of right half of sheet. Brush pasta around mounds of filling lightly with water, then lift left half of sheet and drape over mounds.
- Press down firmly but gently around each mound, forcing out air. (Air pockets increase the chance that ravioli will break during cooking.) Cut pasta (between mounds) with a sharp knife into roughly 2-inch squares. Line a large shallow baking pan with a lightly floured kitchen towel (not terry cloth), then arrange ravioli in 1 layer in it. Make more ravioli with remaining pieces of dough and remaining filling, transferring to lined pan.

- Cook ravioli and Asparagus tips:
- Bring a pasta pot of salted water (2 tablespoons salt for 6 quarts water) to a boil over high heat, then reduce heat to a gentle boil.
- Bring reserved broth to a simmer, then simmer asparagus tips, uncovered, until tender, 2 to 3 minutes. Season broth with salt, then divide broth and asparagus tips among 6 shallow bowls, discarding cheese rind and bay leaf.
- Add half of ravioli to gently boiling water, carefully stirring to separate, and cook, adjusting heat to keep at a gentle boil, until pasta is just tender, 2 to 3 minutes. Lift cooked ravioli with a slotted spoon, draining well over pot, then transfer to bowls with broth. Repeat with remaining ravioli.

120. Four Cheese Ravioli Recipe

Serving: 2 | Prep: | Cook: 15mins | Ready in:

Ingredients

- 2 cup flour
- 1/4 cup butter
- 1 tsp salt
- 1 cup boiling water
- 1 cup ricotta cheese, sieved
- 4 oz parmesan cheese, grated
- 2 oz romano cheese, grated
- 4 oz swiss cheese, grated
- 1 egg, lightly beaten
- 1/2 cup heavy cream
- 2 tbl parsley, finely chopped
- black pepper to taste

Direction

- Prepare the Dough: Put the flour in a bowl. Add the butter in thin slices, then the salt. Stir in the cup of boiling water, and mix together. (I found that it's easiest with an electric mixer or a kitchen aid)
- When the mixture has formed a mass, take it out of the bowl and place on a well-floured board and knead it until it becomes a soft, sticky dough that is rather easy to work and roll out.
- Form the kneaded dough into a ball and place it back in the bowl.
- Cover with plastic wrap so that it does not dry out while it rests.
- Prepare the Filling: In a medium bowl, mix together all ingredients. Taste, and correct for seasoning. If too dry, add a little more cream. Refrigerate until ready to use.
- To Assemble: Clear a large work area and flour the surface well. Keep the flour nearby to dust the work surface and hands as you work. Prepare a lightly floured (enough so that the dried ravioli do not stick to the pan) tray or cookie sheet to put the formed ravioli on.
- Cut the dough in half. Leave half in the bowl and cover with plastic wrap.
- Cut the other half in half again. Roll each piece out about as thin as a penny. Cut the dough into strips about 2 inches by 4 inches.
- Place teaspoonfuls of filling in mounds on each strip. Fold them over so that the squares are now 2x2, with cheese inside.
- Press down on the dough around each mound of filling, then lightly press down on the seal with a fork.
- Repeat with remaining dough.
- Place the sealed ravioli on the prepared tray and cover with a kitchen towel that has been well dredged with flour.
- Let the ravioli sit on the tray for 45 minutes before they are cooked.
- Turn them over every once in a while so that they dry evenly. (The ravioli can be frozen at this point for future use.)
- Bring 6 to 8 quarts of salted water to a boil and drop in 6 to 10 ravioli at a time. Cook 1 minute more after they rise to the surface.
- Remove with a slotted spoon and place them in a warm bowl that has been filmed with melted butter. Pour a little melted butter over the ravioli and keep them warm while you cook the rest. Pour melted butter over each

batch of new arrivals. (Weight watchers can either substitute marg. or eliminate this step)
- Serve with grated Parmesan cheese or tomato sauce.
- Enjoy!

121. Ravioli Lasagna Recipe

Serving: 12 | Prep: | Cook: 1mins | Ready in:

Ingredients

- 1/2 lb sweet Italian sausage
- 1/2 lb hamburger
- 2 pckgs frozen 4 cheese ravioli
- 15 oz. jar spaghetti sauce
- 2 cups shredded Italian cheese blend
- 15 oz. ricotta cheese
- 1/2 cup parmesan cheese
- 1 lrg egg

Direction

- Boil ravioli according to package in a large pot
- Brown hamburger and sausage in a skillet
- Add spaghetti sauce to meat and heat through
- Mix ricotta, parmesan, and egg in medium bowl
- Layer 1/3 of ravioli on bottom of 9 x 13 pan
- 1/2 of cheese and egg mixture
- 1/3 of meat and sauce
- 1/3 of shredded cheese
- Repeat layers again
- Top with the last third of ravioli, meat sauce, and shredded cheese
- Bake at 350 degrees four about an hour or until bubbly

122. Ravioli With Ricotta Sage Filling Recipe

Serving: 4 | Prep: | Cook: 8mins | Ready in:

Ingredients

- 250g ready made pasta dough*, thinly rolled out
- filling
- 200g (homemade) ricotta
- 2 tablespoons grated parmigiano reggiano
- 2 rashers of streaky bacon, cut in small strips (optional)
- 1 tablespoon fresh sage, chopped
- a good hand full dried porcinis, soaked in hot water and chopped
- salt and freshly ground pepper
- *www.marthastewart.com has a foolproof recipe for homemade pasta dough. if you havent got a pasta machine to roll out the dough, simply use a dusted rolling pin (or an empty bottle of wine, depending on how well equipped your kitchen is...)

Direction

- for the filling, place ricotta, grated Parmigiano, sage, chopped porcinis, bacon (optional), a little salt and freshly ground pepper into a bowl and mix (you might find this a little yuck - but its best to do this, using your hands).
- Place readymade pasta dough (in a strip) on a flat surface. Dot 6 piles of filling along one side of each pasta strip and brush around the filling with water. Fold over the pasta dough and press well around each filling to seal. Using a sharp knife cut into ravioli.
- Boil ravioli in salted water for 4-5 minutes until al dente (they will float on top). Drain and drizzle with some olive oil, scatter with some freshly grated parmesan cheese and some leftover herbs like basil, thyme or some fried sage.

123. Rock N Roll Ravioli Lazagna Recipe

Serving: 6 | Prep: | Cook: 20mins | Ready in:

Ingredients

- 1lb of ravioli (frozen or otherwise)
- 1 jar of tomato sauce (whatever flavor you prefer, i just use "traditional")
- 1 container of pesto sauce (or homemade if you prefer)
- 1 jar of alfredo sauce (you won't need the whole thing)
- 1 lb of ground sausage (i usually use jimmy dean)
- 1/2 tsp oregano
- 1/2 tsp basil
- 1/2 tsp savory (if you have it; a lot of people don't)
- breadcrumbs (whatever kind you like and however much you like)

Direction

- 1. As usual, make sure you've got a clean and sterile work environment. I have 4 kids, so "sterile" is a relative term.
- 2. Preheat your oven to 350 degrees.
- In a pan on the stovetop, cook the ground sausage until all the pink is gone.
- 3. Combine the cooked sausage and the marinara sauce in a pot and let simmer.
- 4. In a separate pan, heat your Alfredo sauce (doesn't need to boil, just get it hot).
- 5. Just leave the pesto sauce alone for now. It's not going to escape.
- 6. Boil a pot of water on the stove. Add ravioli. Boil until ravioli is thoroughly not frozen (in fact, you want it hot all the way through).
- 7. Coat a casserole dish (whatever size you have handy, 11x6 works best) with the marinara sauce.
- 8. Line the bottom of the sauce-laden casserole dish with raviolis.
- 9. Cover the ravioli layer with marinara sauce.
- 10. Repeat layering until all of the raviolis and sauce are gone (I got three layers in my pan).
- 11. Ok here's the fun part. You can do this a lot of different ways. Use the Alfredo and the pesto to cover the dish. I do mine in a checkerboard pattern.
- 12. Top with breadcrumbs.
- 13. Place in your preheated oven for 15 minutes (this gets everything all bubbly on top. looks great).
- This goes great with a loaf of French bread with butter and ricotta cheese.

Index

A
Artichoke 4,44
Asparagus 4,65,66

B
Basil 13
Beef 3,4,7,18,24,59
Broth 4,65
Butter 3,4,7,13,28,43,48,50,51,61,64

C
Cheese 3,4,6,8,9,18,20,23,24,31,33,34,35,47,52,59,64,66
Chestnut 3,30
Chicken 3,4,10,11,14,45,58
Chips 4,55
Crab 3,12,13,14
Cream 3,4,14,23,28,31,38,44,47,49,51,52

D
Dumplings 3,12

E
Egg 3,18,30

F
Fat 4,5,33,53,56
Feta 3,20
French bread 68

G
Garlic 3,4,14,49,53,60
Gorgonzola 3,4,23,44

H
Ham 3,24
Hazelnut 3,38
Heart 3,4,25,44

J
Jus 9,59,68

L
Leek 3,24,36
Lemon 4,13,61
Lime 52
Lobster 3,28

M
Mango 4,55
Marsala wine 11
Mascarpone 3,28
Mashed potato 36
Meat 4,56
Molasses 55
Mozzarella 16,42
Mushroom 3,26,30,31,36

N
Nut 4,5,9,23,39,49,63

O
Oil 4,11,49,53
Olive 3,4,33,53,56
Oxtail 4,56

P
Parmesan 4,5,9,10,11,17,22,23,27,28,29,33,36,37,39,40,41,42,43,44,48,49,50,52,53,54,59,62,64,65,67
Parsley 3,10,33
Parsnip 4,55
Pasta 3,7,8,13,15,16,21,32,38,46

Peas 4,44

Peel 18,61,62

Pepper 3,20

Pesto 3,4,14,34,38,39,40,44,49,59

Pie 61

Pomegranate 4,55

Pork 3,27

Port 3,20,36

Potato 3,4,36,61

Prawn 3,36

Prosciutto 4,55

Pulse 15,21,37,54

Pumpkin 3,4,8,37,38,39,55,56

R

Ricotta 3,4,15,23,26,45,47,56,67

S

Sage 3,4,7,28,43,50,51,61,67

Salad 3,9

Salmon 3,4,12,58

Salsa 3,21

Salt 15,51,52,56

Sausage 3,4,15,33,46,51,53,59

Scallop 4,55

Seafood 4,54

Semolina 7,21

Shallot 13

Spinach 3,4,6,7,9,10,11,45,47,59,60,61

Squash 3,4,7,50,51

Stuffing 3,31

T

Taco 4,62

Tomato 3,4,31,63

V

Vegetables 3,33

Venison 4,63

W

Walnut 3,4,7,9,34,46

Wine 4,54

Z

Zest 4,16,64

Conclusion

Thank you again for downloading this book!

I hope you enjoyed reading about my book!

If you enjoyed this book, please take the time to share your thoughts and post a review on Amazon. It'd be greatly appreciated!

Write me an honest review about the book – I truly value your opinion and thoughts and I will incorporate them into my next book, which is already underway.

Thank you!

If you have any questions, **feel free to contact at:** author@cuminrecipes.com

Maria Harris

cuminrecipes.com

Printed in Great Britain
by Amazon